DAN GURNEY

DAN GURNEY

THE ULTIMATE RACER

KARL LUDVIGSEN

Foreword by Sir Jack Brabham

Haynes Publishing

Dedication

For John and Annette Haynes

in pleasure and professionalism

First published in May 2000

British Library Cataloguing in Publication Data:
A catalogue record for this book is available from the British Library

ISBN 1 85960 655 5

Library of Congress catalog card no 99-80193

Published by Haynes Publishing,
Sparkford, Nr Yeovil, Somerset BA22 7JJ.

Tel: 01963 442030 Fax: 01963 440001
Int.tel: +44 1963 442030 Int. fax: +44 1963 440001
E-mail: sales@haynes-manuals.co.uk
Web site: www.haynes.co.uk

Haynes North America Inc.,
861 Lawrence Drive, Newbury Park, California 91320, USA.

Typeset by J. H. Haynes & Co. Ltd., Sparkford

Printed and bound in Great Britain by J.H. Haynes & Co. Ltd

Jacket illustrations
Front cover: Jesse Alexander captures Dan's determination in his first championship Grand Prix race for the Brabham
team at Monaco in 1963. Gurney is among the group battling for the lead when he is retired by a failure of the crown
wheel and pinion.
Back cover: Dan's wave from the cockpit of his Eagle to his many fans at Indianapolis in 1967 is pictured by Stanley
Rosenthall. Although a fuel valve frustrates his Indy attack that year, the months of May and June bring epic success to
Daniel Sexton Gurney.

Frontispiece
As one journalist wrote of Dan Gurney, 'He is a man who knows how to win.' He is enjoying his first and only victory in the
justly celebrated Can-Am series for Group 7 sports cars in 1966 at Bridgehampton, New York.

Contents

Introduction

This may seem a curious admission for an author to make, but this book is incomplete. It couldn't possibly cover the full and ongoing story of the activities and successes of Dan's All American Racers, for example. You can read about AAR's cars and races to 1975 in my book, *Gurney's Eagles*. AAR enjoyed huge success with Toyota power in the IMSA series and was active, still building Eagles, in CART competition through 1999.

Nor could I tell you about the key role that Gurney played in establishing the Long Beach Grand Prix, the first of the modern city-centre races. There wasn't room to mention his challenge to the Grand Prix world to a match-race showdown at the Nürburgring against Gurney in his USAC car with a winner-takes-all prize of $100,000. Interesting that that was never taken up.

Limiting as I have the scope of this book to Dan's personal racing career, I couldn't go into his drive with Brock Yates in Kirk White's Ferrari Daytona to 'win' the Cannonball Baker Sea-to-Shining-Sea Memorial Trophy Dash in November 1971. Dan almost didn't take part, by the way. At first he declined, wrote Yates, mentioning 'pressures from sponsors and how a man in his position shouldn't be out roaring around on the public highway.' But he changed his mind. 'Everybody's terrified of offending somebody,' he told Brock, 'and I almost got caught in that trap.'

As a result, Yates had the rare pleasure of sitting next to a world-class driver as he negotiated the swerving switchbacks of the Prescott National Forest: 'I sat there in admiration, watching him run quickly and easily through the nasty turns, never squealing a tyre, never wasting motion on the steering wheel. Each corner was negotiated with a precision of line that seemed to place the car in perfect position for the next. I had witnessed a virtuoso playing with a fine instrument, and it came to me that this had to be the peak of excellence that every driver must aspire to.'

Yates also came to comprehend the complexity of the person that is Daniel Sexton Gurney. In this book Stirling Moss says of Dan, 'He looks exactly what he is, one of the few human beings I know who does.' Tall, blond and handsome as a matinée idol, Gurney was cast by the racing world as, indeed, an all-American good guy, so much so that cynics in the racing press corps began to refer to him as 'America's sweetheart'.

Unquestioning adulation reached its apogee in the July 1964 campaign by *Car and Driver* magazine to put Dan forward as a presidential candidate. 'Enthusiasts unite!' wrote *C/D*'s editor David E. Davis Jr. 'Join with us in supporting the candidacy of Dan Gurney, running on a platform of unbridled automotive enthusiasm. Gurney – a solid Anglo-Saxon name borne with pride by countless generations of soldiers and men of the soil, merchants and artisans, the very stuff of which America was formed. The name that shall be a rallying cry for thousands of disenfranchised enthusiasts!'

The magazine offered campaign buttons and bumper stickers to its readers and enjoyed a warm response. In November, however, *C/D* had to announce the withdrawal of Dan's candidacy. Belatedly it had 'discovered' that he was two years below the minimum age of 35 years for an American president. Tongue-in-cheek though this candidacy was, it exemplified America's attitude to Gurney. *C/D* said that he was 'in the mould from which all of history's strong, silent American heroes were cast.'

Brock Yates came to know a different Gurney on their cross-country drive: 'He was a complicated man – infinitely deeper than his public image as an affable, all-American nice guy. While he was engaging and easy to reach in public, he was essentially a private person, subject to dark moods and a mercurial temper. For the most part, he used his good looks and easy smile as a shield, letting them serve as representatives of the real Gurney. Even at that, there was a powerful aura of decency and integrity about the man that transcended the perpetual smile and the airy chatter that inevitably arose out of his public interviews. Of the elite of world-ranked drivers, probably none is better liked, and less understood, than Dan Gurney.'

Dan's sense of humour favours horseplay verging in the anarchic – 'gallows humour', he calls it. Wicked practical joking was a staple of the heyday of AAR. Those who saw Dan and A. J. Foyt spraying champagne on the Le Mans podium in 1967 would better have understood if they'd seen Gurney empty a bottle of bubbly over the head of an impeccably-clad Baron Huschke von Hanstein. Or trying a handbrake turn in front of a British pub with a Renault Dauphine, ending up with the car on its side and Mr and Mrs Troy Ruttman with all their luggage tumbling out.

I have been in personal touch with Dan's racing life since he bought my lady an ice cream bar in the paddock at Monza in 1958. As the editor of *Car and Driver* in 1960 and '61 I had a ringside seat for his burgeoning international career. I covered the Can-Am series closely and wrote a book about it. And I was on hand at Indy and Watkins Glen for those crucial years of the birth of the Eagle in the 1960s. Over the decades Gurney and I have had many conversations about cars and racing.

My aim in the creation of this book is to present a pictorial tribute to the career of a great racing driver, accompanied by a text that draws from contemporary sources to tell his story. Dan was a prolific columnist for *Autoweek* and also expressed his views vividly to the AAR Eagle Club, of which I was a proud Charter Member. Sources for these and other quotations from and about Dan Gurney are credited both in the text and in the annotated bibliography, compiled with my thanks by Paul Parker. Because I did not interview or consult Dan specifically for this book, any and all errors of fact or interpretation are solely my responsibility.

I am grateful to all the photographers whose images appear in this book, and especially to Bob Tronolone, who covered so many important aspects of the Gurney career. Special thanks are owed also to Günther Molter, Jesse Alexander, David Phipps, Bernard Cahier and to Stanley Rosenthall, whose fine work we hold in the Ludvigsen Library.

My gratitude goes especially to Darryl Reach and his team at Haynes Publishing for their care and attention to this volume. Most of all I express my thanks to my wife Annette for her love, encouragement and support.

Karl Ludvigsen
Islington, London
April 2000

Foreword

by Sir Jack Brabham

World Champion 1959, 1960, 1966

The first serious competition I remember Dan being in – involved with me – was when he was driving for Porsche. We hit it off right from the start. Obviously Dan was a very good racing driver. I admired his driving and admired him as a man. I also thought he might be a good man to have on our own team one day. Of course if he were racing for us he couldn't be racing against us! So when Porsche quit he joined us in 1963.

We had no team orders at Brabham. 'Dan, you just pass everybody you can!' That was the team order. Dan had the right attitude to racing, which was similar to mine: 'You can be first – after me!' Dan had the same outlook, so that was great. Pretty often, whichever one of us had the better car was out in front. The big challenge for the team was having two cars and getting both of them going as good as they should go.

I enjoyed driving with Dan, because you could get close to him and not worry about whether he was going to lose it. He was in complete control of his car all the time. You could dice wheel to wheel with Dan without any risk. That was important in those days, believe me. Racing was a lot more dangerous then.

I only had one problem with Dan in the team: I had to keep him from tinkering with the car. Dan was very fussy about the way his car was set up. He'd say: 'Move the rear roll bar an eighth of an inch.' Now, not a man in the world would detect the difference an eighth of an inch on a roll bar would make. But, okay, we'd move it an eighth of an inch.

Eventually we realised that it wasn't the car we were setting up at all. We were tuning his brain! After working with Dan for a while, we found that he had to be convinced that the car was as good as he was going to get it. But once we got Dan into gear – satisfied with the set-up of his car – there was no holding him.

It wasn't long before we won our first Grand Prix at Rouen in 1964. I don't remember where I finished; I had a problem with my car. But the pit kept me informed of where Dan was. Dan looked like winning and that was great. It was a fantastic thrill to be there and to see Dan win that first race for Brabham. That was a great day for us all.

Actually, what I was aiming for was retiring from driving and letting Dan take over as number one driver for Brabham. I thought he was the right choice; I wouldn't have had him in the team if I didn't think he was a great driver. I was going to stand down and just worry about the team while he carried on with the driving. That was my idea at the time.

The results were really starting to come. We used to favour Dan with everything. Once when we went to

Dan Gurney (left), Trevor Taylor, and Jack Brabham (right) before the start of the 1964 US Grand Prix. Graham Hill is on the far right.

Monaco we had an engine blow-up and we didn't have any more engines. I gave Dan my engine, and let him race while I watched.

Unfortunately at the end of 1965 he decided he was going to build his own car and drive it. Obviously he had decided well before then, but he didn't tell us. So we were losing him. Now I had to get myself in gear to drive the following year because we didn't have a replacement driver until we got Denny Hulme on board. So I went on driving myself.

Then of course we went on and won the championship two years running, first with myself and then with Denny. We had two very successful years which Dan could have been part of. Dan would have gone on and won the World Championship in our car, several times probably. Of that I'm certain.

I suppose I can't complain, because I won the championship the following year when Dan went off to drive one of his Eagles. It would have been Dan winning the championship instead of me. It turned out all right for me, so I don't mind. I often remind Dan now, of course! I don't let him forget.

Karl Ludvigsen's fine book on Dan's driving career gives me one more chance to remind him!

Jack Brabham

CHAPTER 1

Sixty days in May and June

His thoughts went back to his first such transatlantic trip in 1958. He'd flown in a DC-7 from Los Angeles to Milan with one stop along the way. The big Douglas bird's leather-trimmed seats were deep and comfortable. Its four Wright Cyclone turbo-compound engines droned steadily and reassuringly. That trip took more than a day – hard to imagine in the jet age of 1967, Dan Gurney reflected.

The international commute was now routine for Dan. He first committed himself to it in 1962, the racing season in which he began to mix and match commitments on both sides of the pond in the heart of the busiest months of the racing year. Nor, in his heart of hearts, did he dislike it. He relished the fine engineering of the new generation of jet aircraft, the Boeings and Douglases. Each had its own technology, its own personality. Dan judged the jets worthy of appreciation for their own sake, over and above their function as mere transport.

Dan (36) muffs his start at Spa in 1967 and plummets from the front row to mid-field. This doesn't keep him from coming through to win the Grand Prix of Belgium in his AAR Eagle. This concludes two amazing months for Dan Gurney.

Now, in 1967, he saw merit in these long flights between America and Europe, over the glistening grey snowscapes of Greenland and the cloudy North Atlantic. His company, All American Racers, was just beginning its second year – the one in which many businesses fail. Dan's designer had left and his founding partner was leaving. Combining driving with managing was every bit as challenging as Dan had expected, but no less frustrating for all that.

The successes Goodyear expected after bankrolling AAR had not yet been booked. Even worse, Gurney's 1966 attack on the Indy 500 had been blunted by a crash on the starting line. He'd never even had a chance to win the rich Speedway purse that would have been a boon to his Formula 1 programme, now in its second season. To top it off, his marriage was not in the best of health. Stretching out his six-foot-two-plus frame, Dan took a break at 34,000 feet from the problems that awaited him on the ground.

Before napping he dipped into a book on military history, one of his favourite off-duty topics. Undecided about his career goals after graduating from high school in Manhassett, New York, Dan had taken liberal arts courses at Riverside Junior College and Menlo College in San Francisco, California. Their teachers had failed to fire his interest in history, but his first trips to Europe well and truly lit the flames. He took every chance to explore the histories of the towns and countries he visited. And if he regretted not advancing to higher education – as he sometimes did – he more than made up for it with his voracious reading.

Dan's feelings were positive during this flight to Europe in the first days of May. Two weeks earlier with a Mercury Cougar he had won a Trans-Am race, the Green Valley 300. Fans in the grandstands at the searingly hot Smithfield, Texas, track were waving 'Go Gurney' banners. And he had just left Indianapolis, where he lapped faster than all other contenders at 163.8mph in the practice days after the track opened on 29 April. His 1967 Indy challenge seemed well primed for success.

Landing at Heathrow, Dan travelled to Rye to check on the preparation of the two V-12 Formula 1 Eagles. He and Richie Ginther were entered for the Monaco Grand Prix on 7 May. Arriving at the principality on France's sunny Côte d'Azur, they made their bids to qualify. Dan placed his car eighth on the grid but Richie was half a second over the time needed to squeak into the 16 allowed to start. Frustratingly, AAR was not yet recognised as among the works teams that were guaranteed grid places.

On the Sunday Dan and chief mechanic Tim Wall gave the Eagle its final tweaks. They were the right ones. Dan soon realised that the Eagle was in fine fettle. On the first lap he passed Clark and then Brabham, who was motoring backwards after spinning. Then on successive laps he passed Surtees and Bandini and moved into third behind Denny Hulme and Jackie Stewart. Its V-12 howling, the Eagle handled well over the oily streaks that Brabham's blown engine had laid down.

Suddenly the thrust was gone and all was quiet. Dan rolled to a stop just past the Casino and bounced the car up on the sidewalk. Climbing out, he checked the engine. After only four laps it had broken the small toothed belt that drove the fuel metering unit. Leaning over the car Gurney mused, 'You prepare for a race,

work hard, challenge for the lead, then – bang – it's all over. You stand there by your broken machine wondering why you bother, why the hell can't there at least be another race tomorrow?' Maddening though the failure was, Dan took heart from the engine's strong performance.

On Monday Dan was in the air again and on Tuesday, 9 May, he was back on the track at Indianapolis, where he settled in for qualifying and the race. He lapped at a brisk 164.2mph in his Eagle powered by a four-cam Ford engine that had been modified by AAR's John Miller for added power. Dan also tried an Eagle powered by a Ford with his own Gurney-Weslake pushrod-valve cylinder heads, but decided not to chance qualifying it.

Trackside pundits forecast qualifying speeds in the high 166s. They had to wait to find out on Saturday 13 May because rain squalls pushed back the start of qualifying to 12.48 in the afternoon. Gurney's dark blue number 74 Eagle gradually moved forward in the qualifying queue. Suited up, Dan tugged on his glossy black helmet and slid into its narrow cockpit. Bill Fowler helped buckle him in. The track announcer declared him ready to qualify, and 175,000 fans shouted themselves hoarse. Dan was a favourite to take pole position.

At Indy the average speed for four laps – ten miles – counts. John Miller had tweaked the fuel mixture for maximum power; Dan could feel the added punch as he accelerated through the four gears into turns one and two of the lozenge that is the Speedway. Cool weather suited the engine and the tyres; grip was good and cornering was quick. After his first lap the stentorian tones of announcer Tom Carnegie rolled out over the stands: 'One…six…seven…' The rest was drowned out by the crowd's ebullient surge of sound.

Dan arrowed into the pit lane to the photo and interview spot where he was given his speeds: a best lap of 167.942mph and an average of 167.224 – new records both. Dan was on pole. The driver next up behind him heard the last figure as he pulled out for his run and knew he had his work cut out for him. Mario Andretti had just seen his qualifying speed record broken. He resolved to squeeze all he could from his Brabham-inspired Hawk-Ford. And he did: a four-lap average of 168.982 and a best lap of 169.779mph. Gurney would have to settle for the middle of the front row.

With Sunday qualifying rained out, Dan set to work on the Monday with Bill Fowler and his crew to get two more Eagles ready. During the week he tested the cars for drivers Richie Ginther and Jochen Rindt. Rindt squeezed his on to the last starting row on the weekend but Ginther wasn't happy at the Speedway; Jerry Grant qualified his car instead. On Carburetion Day, 26 May, when teams were finalising their race trim, Dan joined Mario and Parnelli Jones with laps at 163mph. Parnelli was driving the controversial STP-Paxton turbine car with its offset cockpit and four-wheel drive.

Looking through his copy of American motor racing weekly *Competition Press*, Dan read the race forecast of two-times Indy winner Rodger Ward, who said that Gurney 'was long overdue for an Indy win. He is a better driver than most people think he is, and right now I think he has a lot of problems on his mind, like Formula 1, building cars and so on.'

As to the problems, Dan couldn't disagree. Among them was his need for a second driver for his Grand Prix team. Richie Ginther had asked to be relieved of that role, but had agreed to go to England to shake down the F1 Eagles at Goodwood before the next race at Zandvoort. Richie, with Dan and Phil Hill part of the remarkable Californian wave of Grand Prix drivers, would never race again.

Race day, Tuesday 30 May, dawned unusually cold and gloomy for Memorial Day. Dan felt ready to win – but no one knew how the turbine would perform. That question was answered when Mauri Rose pulled aside in the Chevrolet Camaro pace car and released a perfectly aligned field. Dan was edged back by the other first-row racers in Turn One but they were all passed by Jones and the STP turbine from the second row, driving around the outside. Andretti fell back with clutch trouble and Dan moved up to second – 'first in class', he ruefully reflected as he struggled to keep the dayglo-red turbocar in view.

Suddenly his goggles were blurred by raindrops. On his 14th lap the yellow lights came on; they don't race in the rain at Indy. On his 19th lap Dan saw the lights switch from yellow to red. The race was stopped. Cars swerved in and stopped at their pits. Crews broke out their plastic macs and the cars were shrouded while 230,000 spectators sought cover. Hoping to restart, the track management sent out all its rolling stock to try to dry the track. Dan was on their side. With Grand Prix practice starting in Holland on Friday, 'I'd like to get it over with', he said.

Four and a half hours later the rains persisted and the race was abandoned. It would be run on 31 May; Gurney rebooked his flights for a day later. The Wednesday dawned just as unpromisingly but the rains held off and the start – in single-file order – was moved forward to 11.00am. At the restart Dan found he could gain ground ahead of A. J. Foyt, whose Coyote-Ford had challenged the day before, and keep within 5 seconds of Parnelli's whispering turbine. It was fast but vulnerable, Dan knew. In practice it had eaten several drive lines.

The Eagle-Ford was running sweetly and the weather was holding. Although Dan wasn't getting the leader's $150 per lap he consoled himself through lap 40 of the 200 with $50 lap money for the second-place runner. Just before lap 50 he saw the signal from his pits to switch fuel tanks. He'd been burning the methanol in the right-hand tank first to keep as much left-hand weight bias as possible for this anti-clockwise track. Dan reached for the valve's lever and twisted. It didn't budge.

Steering with one hand, Dan twisted the handle with the other. It was still stuck. Ahead, he saw another car spin and, to avoid it, the red turbine spin as well. He was leading! The spin brought out the yellow lights but Jones had the STP car going again and after two laps retook the lead from Gurney – still unable to shift the valve. The right-hand tank would soon be dry. What to do? Before the 60-lap mark Dan dove for his pit. Bill Fowler reached into the cockpit and struggled with the valve, then removed a rear panel to make repairs. After an agonising 5 minutes and 23 seconds Dan was away again – but in 25th place. Worse, a too-lean mixture caused by the fuel valve problem had burned the valves in one cylinder. After mid-race the engine began sounding rough and at three-quarter distance it started smoking enough for the officials to show Gurney the black flag, forcing him to stop.

Back in the AAR garage visitors found a depressed Dan Gurney. The turbine car *did* break three laps from the end, but the man positioned in second to capitalise on that was not Dan but his arch-rival Anthony Joseph Foyt. Winner Foyt was powered by a special V-8 prepared by Ford, the company Dan was trying to beat with its own engine. And to rub it in, Foyt was using Goodyear tyres. AAR had been created by Goodyear to bring it an Indy win; instead Foyt delivered that prize. Worst of all, of the seven Eagles in the field only two finished – one fourth and one ninth. Small wonder that one garage visitor said that Dan 'was making retirement noises'.

Gurney had little time to reflect on the lost opportunity of Indianapolis 1967. On Thursday he flew to Britain and then on to Zandvoort, Holland, for the Dutch Grand Prix. After tests on Friday he felt ready to qualify well on Saturday, 3 June. Although up against the new Lotus-Cosworth in its first race, the Eagle was running well. Graham Hill was quickest in the Lotus, but after checking a gearbox seal Dan turned three laps to set a new practice record of 1:25.1 – chopping 3.6 seconds off the previous year's best.

'I got back in my car,' said Hill afterward, 'and went straight out and equalled this, doing two or three laps at about the same speed; on my last lap, which was also the last lap of practice, I did a 1:24.6 – which set everybody talking.' Dan was back on the track with a changed fuel mixture to make a counter-challenge when the qualifying session ended. Many called it one of the most exciting moments of the Grand Prix season. The race was an anticlimax, with fuel metering problems stopping the Eagle early. After Monaco and Indy, were fuel-feed troubles to be a *Leitmotiv* for 1967?

Dan stayed over at Zandvoort where, on Monday 5 June, New Zealander Bruce McLaren test-drove the Eagle. Bruce was a candidate for the team's open seat. On Tuesday back at AAR's British base Dan led a post-mortem on the Dutch race, where a new, lighter chassis had been raced for the first time. Then he crossed the Channel to Le Mans, where the massive forces of Ford were being marshalled for another attack on the 24-hour race on 10-11 June. Ford had won in 1966 but as part of its commitment to 'Total

Performance' it was back for another bite at the world's premier long-distance race. Gurney was engaged by Carroll Shelby's team of two Mark IV Fords and assigned a surprising co-driver: none other than his Indy arch-rival A. J. Foyt.

Dan knew what the gossip was in the pit lane. 'Some thought it craziness to team Foyt with Gurney,' said a tyre company official. 'They were too competitive of each other. Foyt wasn't at home here as Gurney was.' The sceptics reckoned without Dan's desire to record a Le Mans win in his golden book. In speed around the Le Mans track he could easily have shown up his partner. Gurney was the holder of the race lap record from 1966. But Dan decided on a different tack entirely.

'I knew A. J. pretty well and I think I knew what his problem was going to be,' Dan said later. 'He was in a tough position. He has a tremendous reputation and, yet, when you really get down to it, he *was* in a different world. I told him for sure that Le Mans is not a race, but I could see he didn't quite know that.'

Mutual respect helped Dan and A. J. communicate well during practice. Dan took the responsibility for sorting their red Mark IV Ford, using the baselines set up by Bruce McLaren. Jointly, they agreed on a totally laid-back approach to the race. Dan: 'We feigned no interest in the thing whatsoever. We both felt that this wasn't the most important thing in the world and, yet, we wanted very much to do well. That's the way we worked it: the Indy driver and the road racer on neutral ground.

'I ignored all the hullabaloo that surrounds qualifying,' said Gurney, 'and went out there and ran *slow* – 7 or 8 seconds off the pace. When A. J. finally got in the car – which was very late in practice – I'm sure he was surprised that he could go at my speed so easily. Right there, I think, was a very important part of our being able to win.'

And win they did. They secured the lead against rival Fords, Ferraris and Chaparrals soon after the first hour and never relinquished it. Ferrari driver Chris Amon summed up the common view: 'The Ford that won was the one least likely to finish, because you wouldn't have put money on either Dan or A. J. in a 24-hour race, and they kept up a phenomenal pace. Ferrari had reckoned it would take 128mph to win, but the Ford averaged over 135.'

The atmosphere inside the car reflected the pressure the two Americans applied. Dan was well strapped into Ford Mark IV number J-6 with its special roof bulge for added helmet clearance. 'You're in a hypersensitive state of mind,' said Dan. 'I felt like I had a gallon of adrenaline pumped into me. My nerves were super-raw and they grew 18 feet long from trying to decipher messages coming in from all over the place. The idea, however, was always to cancel out these impressions, to retain control. To pace yourself.

'I'm certain that my eyes must have looked like laser beams,' Dan added. 'It's a real son of a gun about sundown, because there's one spot on the course where the sun slants through the trees right into your eyeballs and makes you blind. You are very aware of the wind, the noise, the change in the attitude of the car as the fuel load runs out and the other traffic, whether it's daylight or night. You're watching your tachometer and your reference points from the lap before. As you're going up through the gears the wind noise increases as you get going faster and faster. And you check your tachometer, which in effect is your speedometer, and you can see how you're doing.'

Dan's fuel bugaboo almost caught them at Le Mans. After four hours Foyt had, in error, been signalled two laps too late to come in for fuel. Approaching the pit straight he felt the engine falter and was just able to drive in to refuel. Said one mechanic to another, 'If Dan had been driving, with his luck it would have happened on the other side of the course.'

Dan admitted that 'I'm supposed to be a jinx at Le Mans.' So when Foyt drove in after his final stint 'it was just a great feeling to see A. J. What can you say to someone at a time like that? I just kept banging him on the shoulder and he was just tickled pink. He might not have been able to let anyone know it, but you knew that winning meant one whale of a lot to him.'

When bottles of champagne were presented to the crews of the top three finishers on the podium the tradition of spraying bubbly by the winners was inaugurated. Reported Jeff Scott, 'Our boy Dan, thumb over the end, shook up his magnum of

champagne like a kid in a soda-pop fight. Whoosh! Grinning from ear to ear, he let fly at everyone within a 20-foot radius. Foyt caught the spirit too and shook up his magnum. Whoosh! Champagne was erupting like Yellowstone geysers. Everyone on the reviewing platform was soaked. The announcer called out "... *Le vin bain, Americain!*"' 'I could tell Henry Ford II had mixed emotions when we were spraying champagne all over everybody on the victory platform after the race,' Dan recalled. 'The spraying wasn't very selective, you see.'

Dan had little time to reflect on this success. The next Grand Prix was the following weekend at Spa in Belgium. Back in Britain on Tuesday 13 June he was at Goodwood for another Bruce McLaren test. Bruce was happy with the car but engine problems meant that only one Eagle would race at Spa. There on Friday Dan had only to turn a couple of laps of the daunting 8¾-mile road course to know that he needed a change of gear ratios.

'The secret of Spa,' said Gurney, 'is to make no violent moves. No sudden braking, no sudden sharp turns that can get you into trouble. Actually, it's controlled violence that does it. The real thrill comes in the downhill curves, where the G forces push your whole stomach over against your rib cage. This is it: this is the Olympics compared to an ordinary track meet.' His Friday time split the Lotus-Fords on the front row of the Spa grid and was equalled on the Saturday. A good race was in prospect.

Dan was in a relaxed frame of mind at the Goodyear cocktail party after the Saturday practice. He mixed easily and affably with the European racing press, who saw a lot to admire in this determined and experienced American. One engaged him with a lengthy and earnest dissertation to which Dan replied with a typical Gurneyism: 'There's a lot of right in what you say ... even though you're wrong!'

After its misty dawn race day, 18 June, was blessed with sun. Engrossed in last-minute preparations, Dan missed the driver's meeting. This proved almost calamitous. He had not been told – as the others had – that the starting flag would be waved at any time after the 30-second board.

Dan did not pretend to be relaxed: 'Sitting waiting for

a start I don't think of anything much. I'm keyed up, and I'm waiting to put my racing plan into practice. I'm not scared, and I'm not concentrating so hard that I can't hear anything but race sounds. Any race is a thrill and waiting to start is part of that.' Coming down from the dummy grid, the cars poised on the start line – and were quickly flagged away. Except for D. S. Gurney, who was not in gear. Hastily grabbing first, Dan got away in the first half-dozen.

On the second of 28 laps Gurney moved into third behind Jim Clark's Lotus-Ford and Jackie Stewart's BRM. The Eagle V-12's titanium exhaust pipes were howling. Routine was shattered on the 12th lap when Jim Clark pitted for spark-plug attention and Dan halted briefly at his pit to shout 'Fuel pressure!' Fuel troubles again! For several laps Dan had seen his fuel pressure falling. He was sure it was the end of another race. 'I thought I was running out of gas. I was starving down the straights. I didn't expect the car to last. I was trying to figure out, "Is it better if I do full throttle or part-throttle, or what?"'

By then Dan was second and could see Jackie Stewart's big BRM H-16 ahead: 'I saw a wisp of oil coming out of his car and said to myself, "Oops, this guy may have himself a problem."' Thought Dan, 'Either my car's going to blow or it's not going to blow, but it's no use blowing it if I'm not gassing it all the way. Two laps later, I went by him. He was having gearbox trouble. My problem just straightened itself out. I could

hardly believe it. I could have run the car even faster if I hadn't worried so much about that.'

As for speed, Dan had to make no excuses. He set a new record fastest lap at 148.8mph and his race average of 146.0mph was also a record. His winning margin was 63 seconds. On the podium for the second Sunday in succession, he displayed 'a vast Gurney-type grin that almost had his ears falling in the ends.' Hearing 'The Star-Spangled Banner' was evocative: this was the first victory by an American driver and car in a national Grand Prix since Jimmy Murphy beat all comers in a Duesenberg at Le Mans in 1921.

With no champagne to distribute, Dan stripped the flowers from his victory wreath and tossed them to the crowd. He was hustled off to appear on Belgian television. The prize-giving followed, and the day concluded back at his hotel with a relaxed dinner with his team, Goodyear people and some press friends. It had been a great day for Gurney and he had no intention of rushing it to a conclusion.

Sixty days in May and June had ended with wonderful successes in France and Belgium. It had not – as we have seen – been achieved without wholehearted and profound commitment on the part of Dan Gurney. 'As a personal milestone, and an achievement for the whole team, Spa meant a great deal,' Dan reflected. 'It said that despite all the odds, we'd done it. I guess you could say that that was the high point of my racing career.'

A. J. Foyt (left) and Gurney celebrate a victory for Ford and Goodyear at Le Mans in 1967. Judged unlikely by many, the pairing of two American racing legends succeeds thanks to Gurney's canny pre-race strategy.

Dan is in pensive mood (left) as he inspects the entrails of his Eagle V-12 at Monaco in 1967. Its fuel injection will let him down in the race. At Indianapolis he is interviewed for ABC Television's Wide World of Sports *by Jim McKay (above). Dan's crew blankets the Indy Eagle-Ford before the 1967 500-mile race (opposite), from which he must retire after problems with a balky fuel valve. Gurney's honour is intact, however, after a record-breaking qualifying run to the centre of 1967's front starting row (overleaf) between Mario Andretti (1) and Gordon Johncock (3).*

At a pit stop for the big Ford Mark IV on its victory at Le Mans in 1967 (left and above) Gurney and Foyt compare notes with cowboy-hatted Carroll Smith while between them is AAR engine man John Miller. Necktie-wearing Teddy Mayer looks down on the tableau. After the race Bernard Cahier snaps Gurney and Foyt with the hard-working Goodyear tyre team.

A tradition is born at Le Mans in 1967 when Dan Gurney, between Mike Parkes (left) and Foyt, pops the cork of a magnum of Moët, relishes the overflow and commences spraying the contents on all and sundry including Index of Performance winners Hans Herrmann and Jo Siffert (at right opposite).

Dan Gurney's amazing 60 days in May and June of 1967 culminate with his victory at Spa in the Eagle-Weslake V-12. He sits thoughtfully in the car, remonstrates with second-place finisher Jackie Stewart, cleans the grime from his face and stands solemnly to hear the strains of 'The Star-Spangled Banner'. Dan would later describe this as the high point of his racing career.

CHAPTER 2

By Ferrari to Ferrari

'*Who is that great driver?*' Spectators on that grey November Sunday at Riverside leafed feverishly but vainly through their programmes. They found the entrant of the loud red number 69 4.9-litre Ferrari, Frank Arciero, well-known Montebello building contractor. But there was no mention of his car's driver. Yet here he was, leading the main event ahead of an elite field that included Carroll Shelby, Walt Hansgen, Richie Ginther, Masten Gregory and Paul O'Shea, all piloting very respectable equipment.

Driving a Maserati 450S, in 1957 by far the most powerful sports-racing car available, Shelby led early but spun. The lead was seized by the unknown newcomer piloting the Arciero Ferrari. His speed on the long straight was a record-setting 163mph. Shelby caught him, but passing him was another matter. The Ferrari fended off Carroll's advances until five laps from

Dan Gurney discovers early that the awesome Arciero 4.9-litre Ferrari demands his total concentration at all times. He starts from pole at Pomona, California, in March 1959 but retires with engine troubles.

the end of the 25-lap race. Dan Gurney – for it was he – finished 5 seconds behind Shelby.

Few drivers have made more of a reputation by finishing second than Dan Gurney. The crowd around his Ferrari in the paddock was immense. And when he and his wife walked into the ballroom at the Mission Inn for the prizegiving that evening he received a standing ovation. Winner Shelby was generous in his praise for the tall, blond, good-looking 26-year-old, who was – astonishingly – competing in only his 13th auto race. The 13th official, sanctioned auto race, that is, for Gurney had been racing on the roads for years.

'The first attraction was as a fan,' Dan told Dale Kistemaker. 'I was smitten at a very early age. Racing always did something for me. The next thing was getting my own licence, then going out and actually driving. I remember going by myself to a triangular-shaped dirt road and just making all kinds of mistakes. It was what I wanted to do, a tremendous thrill.' Young Gurney had been bitten badly by the automotive bug at Manhassett High School on New York's Long Island. Hanging out with an older crowd already well-equipped with cars, he was exposed early to their attractions.

Born on 13 April 1931, Dan Gurney was already well aware of the appeal of automobiles. Machinery was in the family. In 1905 his paternal grandfather had established the Gurney Ball Bearing Company to make specialised bearings for many purposes, including vehicles. Its New York state factories are still in business as an arm of Sweden's SKF. Although Dan's father, John R. 'Jack' Gurney, was successful in the physics studies he was obliged to pursue, his fine bass voice won him an operatic career instead. Dan's middle name, Sexton, was the maiden name of his mother Roma; the couple were married in 1929.

Dan would never forget that when the Vanderbilt Cup races were run in 1936 and '37 a scant seven miles from his Port Jefferson home, 'I didn't get to see them. I came within a few hundred yards, but my folks wouldn't let me in. I have been getting revenge ever since!' He read Floyd Clymer's reprints of George Monkhouse's books about racing: 'His famous book *Motor Racing with Mercedes-Benz* always had a special attraction for me – road racing versus oval racing. I used to read about those races and think, "Gee, that would be a good thing for the States."'

Dan started tinkering with engines – model airplane engines at first. News of hot-rod doings came his way from mimeographed newsletters passed around at school. Real racing American-style was on view at the Freeport oval track on the south coast of Long Island. Dan and his friends often watched the stock cars there and especially the snarling midgets, where a driver from his home town used the pseudonym 'Ted Tappet' to win race after race. 'Tappet', better known as Phil Walters, later put his skills at the disposal of the Briggs Cunningham team and became one of the outstanding road racers of the 1950s.

'My first car was a '33 Ford roadster,' Dan told Phil Llewellin. 'I sent away for a two-carburettor manifold and did a few other things to it, including rebuilding the engine in a parking lot, where a milk truck ran over the crankshaft.' But hod-rodding on Long Island was a pale imitation of the real thing, then booming in the California to which the Gurneys – with Dan's younger sister Celissa – moved in 1948. Jack Gurney's inheritance on the death of his father in 1947 prompted

a passion for avocado farming, to which their new acreage at Riverside, east of Los Angeles, was ideally suited.

For a car-crazy teenager California was a dream come true: 'It was like being thrown into a briar patch. Just great. As early as 1950 I was on the salt at Bonneville with my own hot rod. I turned 130.43mph, using a Mercury flat-head which I'd modified. I had that old Merc in a lot of cars before I finally got rid of it.' Drag racing was his sport of choice, he told Jim McFarland: 'We ran on a few of the early strips, even before Santa Ana started up. We had this triangle-shaped track for drags, and you could race three times going around if you wanted, but the Marine Corps came in and kicked everybody out.'

These were the outlaw years of hot-rodding before organised drag racing began, Dan recalled for Barrie Gill: 'Bands of us would go from town to town, pull into a drive-in restaurant and take on the local boys. It was pretty exciting. You could end up with 25 or 30 cars. They'd be racing in both directions with lots of people on the side pulling transmissions out because they'd blown their gears. Then the police would arrive – converging with about eight or ten cars at once with all the lights going. Everybody just scattered. That's when you needed your acceleration – and brakes!'

His contemporaries had already marked Dan Gurney as a man to watch, friend Perry Bronson told Steve McNamara: 'We had laid out a home-made track outside of town. Dan came out in what I remember was a stock '40 Ford. Most of us had pretty hot roadsters and we knew the track pretty well. Dan came out there and he drove like there was no tomorrow. Everybody thought, "This is it!"'

Hot-rodding was cost-effective for a cash-strapped teenager but European-style road racing still attracted Dan: 'Right away road racing appealed to me. Road racing is real driving – it's related to driving on a regular road in a regular car. I liked dragging and record runs, but there was something that I missed in those that road racing seemed to offer. I felt that it asked more of the car. There seemed to be more inventiveness and engineering involved. You had whole factories competing against each other rather than private individuals all running the same kinds of concepts. It just seemed far more exciting with more scope and tradition. And the international aspect of road racing interested me.'

Road racing was getting under way in California then under the aegis of the California Sports Car Club. The Sports Car Club of America was also involved, but it was more of an East Coast movement and competition between the American coasts was as active then as now. Dan's first sight of a road race up north at Pebble Beach in 1950 did nothing to discourage him. But professional road racing in America was still unknown; trophies were the only rewards. Dan nurtured the dream of making a living as a driver but reality dictated otherwise.

In the autumn of 1952, with a war on in Korea, Gurney decided to deal with his obligation to the Army. 'I didn't have to go into the service,' he told Peter Manso, 'but I volunteered for the draft to get it out of the way, because I didn't really know what I wanted to major in at college.' He trained as an anti-aircraft gunner and arrived in Korea with the Eighth Army a few months before the cease-fire was negotiated in July 1953. 'I never saw any real action,' he admitted to Barrie Gill, 'except for taking a few shots at our own airplanes when they weren't identified right.'

Dan was philosophical about his two years in the service: 'When I was in the Army I didn't like it one minute but now that I look back I wouldn't trade it for anything. It makes me feel good to know that I've been through it.' With that behind him at 23, Dan Gurney made other commitments. He took a job at Hunter Engineering in Riverside and settled down there with bride Arleo Bodie. Soon young Gurneys arrived, first son Johnny and then daughter Lyndee. Later the couple would produce two more sons, Dan and Jim.

While Dan was away, road racing had boomed with new tracks and cars. A friend from hot-rodding days, Skip Hudson, was as besotted as Dan. Together they schemed to break into the charmed circle of the sport where fellow Californians like Phil Hill and Richie Ginther were already ensconced. 'Through their connections with various people, primarily but not just with John von Neumann, they were off and running.

They had a support system. That was a hard rung to reach for, but that was our goal. And like all good competitors if they could kick your hands off the rung of the ladder, they'd do it, naturally! Of course!'

Dan started on the bottom rung with a used Triumph TR2 bought from motorcycle dealer Joe Vittone. Already well broken in with 18,000 hard miles, the Triumph was immediately entered for a race at Torrey Pines on 23 October 1955. Its eager driver hadn't yet mastered heel-and-toe downshifting: 'I had a heck of a time getting slowed down and into the proper gear for the corners. You'd come to the end of the straightaway and there'd be this silence – and then *crunch, crunch, crunch*!' Race preparation also had to be mastered: 'When it was over, the wheels were so loose you could turn the lug nuts with your fingers.'

After another race at Palm Springs in December – he stuffed the TR2 into a hay bale to avoid a spinning competitor – Dan 'realised that it was going to be difficult to be recognised. No matter how well you did it wasn't particularly noticeable' when you were piloting a humble Triumph. Skip Hudson had already upgraded to a 1955 Porsche Speedster and Dan followed suit with a '56, trading in his TR2 and paying $100 a month to the bank. 'They probably didn't realise what I was going to be doing with it.'

What he did with it was race Hudson at every opportunity. Wrote Steve McNamara, 'Dan and Skip found a subdivision outside Riverside which had streets, lights, fire plugs – everything but houses and people. Night after night, week after week, they raced through the empty streets, tuning their reflexes, developing their touch.' 'We slammed our cars around turns,' said Dan, 'skidded them, downshifted – and had ourselves many a two-man Porsche race. We both learned plenty.'

Although the Riverside police felt otherwise, these outings were not just hooligan antics by men in their mid-20s. Gurney: 'Skip and I took an oath that we would never not tell ourselves the truth on a stopwatch. Regardless of how painful it may have been. Wherever we went we used a stopwatch to see how we compared, because in the end that's terribly important. We'd set up segments and do laps there, on the dirt, and time each other.'

Gurney and Hudson did likewise on the road circuits in Southern California. Sometimes they would sneak into a track: 'We were there when the bulldozers were building Riverside.' And if you knew which motel to stop at on the way north out of Palmdale you could borrow the key that unlocked the padlock that held the chain that kept people from driving unbidden on to the track at Willow Springs. 'And we did that.'

They also became initiates into the exotic world of Porsche racing. 'We befriended two Porsche stalwarts,' Dan recalled. One was Rolf Wütherich, the expert Porsche mechanic who survived the crash in which James Dean was killed. 'They were super enthusiasts about Porsche and infected us with their enthusiasm. They taught us how to set the float levels, how to adjust the torsion bars to lower the ride height and put on Englebert tyres. So we had cars that could actually get around the track pretty doggone well.'

The effort paid off. Dan won his production-car class in his first Porsche race at Santa Maria in July 1956. He did well in three other races that summer and autumn but found the cost crippling: 'I learned that racing even as an amateur costs a great deal of money if you want to win, but I learned also that it was great fun. After four events I was tapped out. It had me in the poor house. The answer was to get to drive someone else's car.' That transition, Gurney found, was 'very, very difficult.'

Dan cadged one race in a Porsche owned by Mory Kassler and another in Louise Bryden-Brown's Denzel, a Porsche-like roadster. By courtesy of Elliot Forbes-Robinson he even had an outing in a Lancia Aurelia Spyder – 'I managed to spin that in a very awkward place. But it was a nice passenger car and I appreciated getting a chance to drive it.' With a half-dozen other racing hopefuls Dan had an audition early in 1957 at Willow Springs for the racing stable run by Tony Parravano, which included many Italian exotica. In spite of lapping fastest by far in a Ferrari Mondial, Dan was shown the gate for an off-course excursion that punctured its fuel tank. He kept the offending rock as a souvenir.

Later that summer Dan Gurney had a better outing at Willow, one that 'really broke the ice' for a driver who wanted – indeed needed – to be noticed. As they'd done so often he and Skip Hudson drove up to the demanding, hilly road circuit to see what was afoot. They found a couple of fellows test-running a white Corvette. Famous though it was later to become as a production racing car, Chevrolet's Corvette was a relatively little-known quantity in 1957. And these drivers were struggling to master quirks that had them spinning off the track.

Summoning all his reserves of cheek, Dan ambled over to them. 'Look,' he said, 'why don't I try it to see if the car's okay?' Amazingly, they agreed. 'How I managed to do that I don't know,' Dan recalled, 'but I got in the thing and promptly found out that it had a funny tweak. It spit me off the road as well. But I recovered from that and ended up running what was a new lap record for a Corvette at Willow Springs.'

Unbeknownst to Dan, one of the Corvette drivers, Cal Bailey, worked for a car-crazy building contractor, Frank Arciero. Arciero had a small stable of racing cars that were driven by Bob Drake, among others, and Bailey had a new black race-prepared Corvette of his own. Much in demand, Drake was slated to drive it one Sunday at Riverside, 22 September 1957, but had a conflict with another commitment. After the record laps at Willow Bailey thought, 'Why not Gurney?' Dan seized this opportunity with both gloved hands.

'I managed to get the job done there,' said Dan. He led all the Corvettes, Jaguars and 300SLs at Riverside and won the big production-car race with a margin at the finish of a second less than half a minute. Would he like to drive the car in the main event for modified cars as well? 'Absolutely, yeah!' Finishing sixth overall – as he did – was a fine result for a stock Corvette.

Gurney was now a bigger blip on the Southern California radar screen. His buddy Skip Hudson had been heightening his own profile as well. Both drivers were weighed by Frank Arciero to try to tame a cranky sports-racing Ferrari he had bought from the Parravano stable. The 4.9-litre car was fast – clocked at 179mph at Bonneville – but declared by driver after driver to be unmanageable. Maybe a new driver was the answer, mused Arciero. He asked the respected Richie Ginther about Hudson and Gurney. Which would be his choice? Richie gave Gurney the higher rating.

Arciero's call to Gurney was clear: 'Would you like to come up and test this 4.9 Ferrari at Willow Springs?' Knowing well the car's 'evil reputation', Dan decided to start with the basics. He took the car to Willow's paved parking area and proceeded to spin it on the throttle a few times to get a feel for its traction – or lack of it. This flabbergasted Arciero and his mechanic. 'What kind of nutcase are we dealing with?' they asked each other. Then Dan took to the track.

'It didn't want to put the power on the ground,' Gurney found. 'You couldn't come off a corner with the tail out and expect to get anywhere. It would just spin the tyres. So you had to adapt to it. You had to "diamond" the corner, get the turn over with and be going more or less straight in order to accelerate.' Probing the limits of the Ferrari's chassis, Dan found a way to gear it to the road. He did so, in fact, so well that he set a new absolute lap record for Willow. It looked like Arciero had a new driver.

Gurney's next drive was his epic second place behind Carroll Shelby at Riverside in November 1957. Next time out in December at Paramount Ranch he won overall, defeating 15 others in an hour-long race. *Road & Track* hailed the winner: 'Gurney's rise to local fame has been, to put it tritely, meteoric.' April and May 1958 saw him win twice more in the big Ferrari, at Palm Springs defeating Carroll Shelby in a similar car. Dan didn't kid himself: 'Carroll could outdrive me at that time. As he can be, Carroll was very nice to this new young guy coming along. He kind of praised me, and that was a big boost.'

Polished though his performance looked from the outside, in the cockpit Gurney was on a steep learning curve with the Ferrari: 'I found out something in that Ferrari,' he told Robert Cutter and Bob Fendell: 'I found that the better you can concentrate while driving, the better lap times you have. It was also a different sensation. All the cars I had raced before this were tame and quiet. This Ferrari felt as if I had to hang on for dear life to control it. I couldn't take my attention away from it for a second.'

In one of his races Dan came up against a Kurtis being driven by Mickey Thompson, who well remembered the encounter: 'I had had a lap-after-lap battle with one of the most determined drivers I have ever encountered. He was in a big, ill-handling Ferrari and it was beautiful to see how his smooth handling skill overcame the car's vices. I thought, "*Man*! That kid is going to be a great driver!"'

Dan would drive Arciero's number 69 Ferrari in a few more races in 1958 and '59 but never with the blazing success of that 1957-58 winter. At Tracy in Northern California he raced a Maserati 450S for John Edgar in May of '58 but retired with tyre trouble. Twice in March of that year he found himself in a Ferrari 250GT coupé. Early in the month he finished fourth overall with one in an airport race near Phoenix, Arizona. Later in March Dan competed in Sebring, Florida's 12-hour race, sharing a little French DB coupé with Howard Hanna. During practice, however, he took four laps in another 250GT under the critical gaze of Ferrari's man in America, Luigi Chinetti.

Noticed though he was, Dan Gurney was no closer to his goal of a professional race-driving career. Where prize money was paid it was not a lot: 'Maybe $350 or a nice trophy, pot-metal trophy. But, you know, we were in heaven.' Earthly needs had to be satisfied, however. Dan was donating his services as a mechanic to Dick Pruitt and Bill Fowler of the Arciero team, 40 miles away in Los Angeles. Between this and his racing he was short-changing his Riverside employer, Hunter, for whom he had managed the successful launch of a continuous-casting machine for aluminium. It's either racing or us, said Hunter. Choosing racing, Gurney was terminated by Hunter.

This, early in 1958, was a low point for Dan and his family: 'very traumatic – almost like a failure. I applied for and went and received unemployment. I stood in line to get my cheque. It was awfully hard on my pride.' He only had to do this once, however. Dan received a phone call from Luigi Chinetti. An Italian who had lived for many years in France and now in New York, Chinetti was famously incomprehensible in all his languages. But this time his message was clear: would Dan like to drive for his North American Racing Team at Le Mans? 'Naturally I declined!' joked Gurney.

Dan spent the summer in Europe. At both Le Mans and later in a Reims 12-hour race his Ferraris were crashed by his co-drivers. Making the rounds of the races he teamed up with another tall American racer, Troy Ruttman, and his family. The precocious Ruttman had become the youngest-ever winner of the Indy 500 in 1952 when he was only 22. 'I knew he was a gifted race driver,' Gurney recalled. 'As a spectator watching him you could tell he was something very special. But by the time he came on this trip he had been through an awful lot. He was on a downhill slide in his career. But he was still enormous fun to be with. He told me a lot about Indy Car racing and racing philosophy in general.'

He and Ruttman had their first sight of the Nürburgring, where they practised in a Renault Dauphine whose loan had been arranged by photojournalist Bernard Cahier. Bernard was the link with Guglielmo 'Mimmo' Dei's Scuderia Centro Sud. 'Dei knew everybody in Modena,' Dan said. He and Cahier arranged for Gurney to drive a 1,500cc Osca in a sports car race at the 'Ring: 'I didn't even realise then that the Maserati brothers were behind Osca. But it was a great-looking car and it had a nice-performing engine.'

Dan placed seventh behind the silver Porsches and Borgwards in the sports car race. 'I didn't even see 'em after the race started,' Gurney recalled. 'But I kept my head down and was trying to drive this circuit. Every little experience you could get in those days at that place was well worth it. They were very pleased. They said that I'd driven an Osca nearly 20 seconds a lap quicker than anybody else had ever done. It was kind of narrow and high and I got it up on two wheels, bicycling, a couple of times. It was a damn nice car, but it wasn't a very good bicycle!'

For the eager Gurney the summer was rich in revelatory sights and experiences. Thanks to Mimmo Dei he lapped the Modena Autodromo in a Maserati. He saw racing at Monza and Silverstone as well as the Nürburgring and Reims: 'I was at the 'Ring the day Peter Collins was killed, driving a Ferrari. I saw Musso killed at Reims, driving a Ferrari. And I'm thinking, "Boy! I can't *wait* to get into this!" The desire to race overcame all those concerns.'

Dan was stunned by the challenge offered by Europe's road courses: 'What struck me most when I got to Europe were the blind turns. I was really shocked. You just don't make any mistakes there. On most tracks in the States you could see where you were going and drive accordingly. European racing involved a lot of blind curves. If you lose it on one of those European circuits, things can get pretty serious. You had to get to know the track in precise detail and make critical decisions based on that knowledge.'

Back from Europe, Dan raced in the eastern USA for the first time at Watkins Glen, New York, at the end of September. In a *Formule Libre* race won by Jo Bonnier's Maserati 250F, he was second in a 3.5-litre Ferrari sports car fielded by Luigi Chinetti's team. At Chicago's Meadowdale he raced a Ford stock car until its clutch gave out. Then back at Riverside in October Dan drove the Arciero Ferrari to second behind Chuck Daigh's Scarab.

Something resembling a professional racing career was beginning to materialise for Dan Gurney. After Riverside he was relaxing at his nearby home when 'the phone rang. Chinetti was on the other end.' Was it news of another drive? Perhaps Nassau in the Bahamas? The familiar rasping tones conveyed quite a different message: 'He said that Enzo Ferrari himself had asked me to make a personal test and asked if I could leave at once for Modena in Italy. The plane ticket was ready and waiting for me. I whooped and yelled. My wife must have thought I'd gone crazy. It was a fantastic break.'

Dan discusses the daunting challenge of the Nürburgring with Troy Ruttman, his travelling companion in the summer of 1958. Indy racer Ruttman is out of his league in the Scuderia Centro Sud Maserati 250F, which is a non-starter after failing its engine in practice.

In four photos taken at the Pomona, California, Fairgrounds track in February and March of 1959, Bob Tronolone captures the aggressive Gurney style at the wheel of the awesome Arciero Ferrari. Its non-original body was built in California by transplanted Englishman Jack Sutton.

At the start of the Los Angeles Examiner Grand Prix in Pomona in March 1959 (overleaf) Gurney leads a fabulous field of sports-racers including the Buick-powered special of Max Balchowsky (70), Carroll Shelby's Maserati (98), Chuck Daigh in a Kurtis-Buick (6) and just behind him Billy Krause in another V-8 Maserati. Chasing them is a gaggle of California's finest.

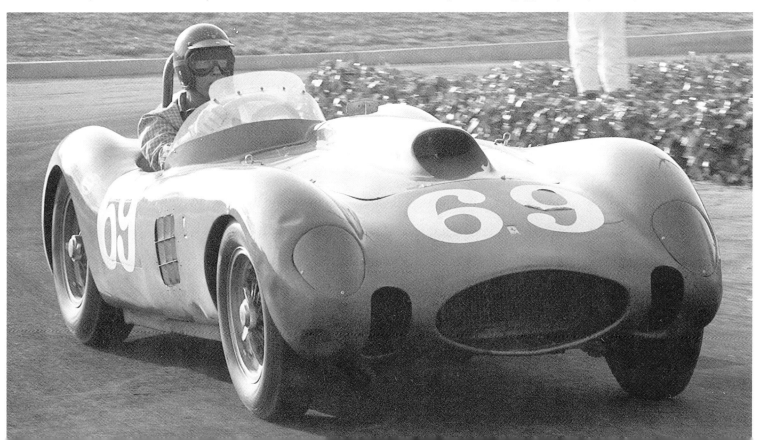

In the 1,500cc sports car race at the Nürburgring in August 1958 Gurney finishes seventh with an Osca behind the silver factory squads of Porsches and Borgwards. He finds that the relatively high-built Osca has a tendency to 'bicycle' at times. With his all-American good looks, immense enthusiasm for motor racing and sponge-like ability to absorb information about his chosen career, Dan Gurney's is a welcome new face in the international motor racing world of 1958 and '59.

CHAPTER 3

Grand Prix passions

Yes, I did recommend Dan Gurney to Ferrari. I don't know why. If I had any sense I would have said, "No, I don't think Gurney should be here." Why would anybody possibly want, on the same team, the guy that stood to show him up the worst? Did Prost want Senna to come and be a part of the team?' Phil Hill shook his head, recalling this for Tim Considine. Having raced in America against Dan, four years his junior, Phil respected the skill and determination of his fellow Californian. Defying expectation, Phil didn't kick Dan's hands off that rung of the ladder. On the contrary: he offered a hand up.

Phil Hill was hospitable to Dan in 1958, his first season in Europe. 'A fellow American looked mighty nice to see when you're over there feeling pretty alone and not really speaking the language very well,' Gurney remembered. 'Phil helped a lot.' Also in Europe that 1958 season was American driver-reporter Denise McCluggage; the three of them teamed up for Dan's first visit to Modena.

Gurney's last drive for Enzo Ferrari is at Monza on 13 September 1959. He finishes fourth in a Ferrari Dino that he feels is slightly lacking in the horsepower department.

Dan's next trip to Modena – in November of 1958 at the invitation of Luigi Chinetti – was altogether different. No friendly face awaited him. He was set an initiative test to find his own way to Modena from the Milan airport. Once settled at the Albergo Reale he waited two long and stress-enhancing days before receiving any word about the test for which he had flown to Italy. On the third morning he was at the Modena Autodromo by appointment. The sky was cloudy and the air cool over the flat circuit on the town's periphery, tracing a small airport's perimeter road. The big red Ferrari transporter rolled up with three racing cars – all to educate and evaluate Daniel Sexton Gurney.

Three black Fiats followed. Dan: 'All these men got out of their Fiats. They wore dark overcoats and fedora hats and had their collars turned up because it was cool. It looked very mysterious and official, like a movie version of a Mafia get-together. Among them was Enzo Ferrari himself and the racing engineers and the regular racing mechanics, who were unloading all three cars. They had a 2-litre sports car, a 3-litre sports car and a 2½-litre Grand Prix car. I drove the cars in that order.

They decided how many laps I did and I didn't do more than ten laps in each one. You don't have much time to get familiar when you drive three different cars. Time is very limited.'

Dan found out later that he'd done what they wanted: turned progressively faster laps without spinning. His best lap in the Formula 1 car was 62 seconds when the Autodromo lap record was around 59 seconds to the credit of Jean Behra in a similar car. Gurney drove the car that Mike Hawthorn had raced; its roomy cockpit easily accommodated him.

Hawthorn had retired after winning the 1958 Formula 1 world championship. In what was otherwise a ghastly season for Enzo Ferrari, both Luigi Musso and Peter Collins were killed in his cars. Phil Hill, who had driven his first Grands Prix for Ferrari at the end of 1958, was still aboard. Frenchman Jean Behra and Briton Tony Brooks were recruited by Ferrari from BRM and Vanwall respectively for 1959. This seemed a strong team, but it was unproven. Added strength would also be needed for sports car races. Thus – the presence of Dan Gurney at the Autodromo.

Not a word was said to Dan about how well or poorly he did. Mino Amorotti was there, the engineer who represented Ferrari at the races. He said, 'Okay, tomorrow you and our test driver, Severi, are going to Monza.' They arrived to find not only clouds but heavy rain. Visor at the ready, Dan took the wheel of the Testarossa sports car after Severi set a bogey time. 'Martino Severi was never a great race driver but he was a very good test driver,' said Dan, 'and he certainly knew his way around Monza!

'I got into this car and I didn't fit. The seat was too tight and my knees were up around my ears.' Even worse, Dan had a wad of lire notes in his hip pocket. Cutting off his circulation, it put his throttle foot to sleep after a couple of laps. Nevertheless he succeeded in matching Severi's time through the mist and rain. 'After they finally called me in, I spun the car on the cool-off lap. It didn't go off the road. I never said a word about it and I don't know if anybody ever knew it. That was the end of my second day of tests for Ferrari.'

Although Gurney went back to California not knowing how Ferrari rated him, he felt as though he

had achieved something in the tests: 'I felt that I was going to get a chance.' The chance materialised in a telegram that said in essence: 'We'd like you to drive on the sports car team, starting at Sebring and after that the Targa Florio and the thousand kilometres at the Nürburgring.' Dan was to receive one return-trip air ticket and the equivalent of $163 a month with no guarantee that he would race – but half the starting and prize money if he did. 'So naturally I signed up immediately! I figured that I would make it. I ended up making $7,600 in 1959, which was enough to exist on pretty well in those days.'

'In June 1959, after competing in three sports car races for Ferrari, Dan was asked to attend a test at Monza. Behra was testing the latest evolution of the Formula 1 car: 'They said, "You might get a chance to drive it." No promises.' After Jeannot set a new Formula 1 record for Monza Dan was offered the wheel. He had refreshed his recollection of the circuit – experiencing it for the first time in the dry – with a few laps in his Volkswagen.

'Finally, late in the day, I was given my chance,' Dan recalled. 'I liked the car, although it wasn't quite as user-friendly as I had imagined it would be. It wasn't the sort of car that invited you to take liberties. You had to be reasonably precise and careful with it, as opposed to one where you could get it sideways and hoof it and opposite-lock it and that sort of thing. It didn't like that. Nevertheless if you bore down and tried to extract every last little bit from it, it would stand up to it. It would pay off.' Gurney's tactics in taming Arciero's 4.9-litre were turning out to be useful.

'Within ten laps I was able to break Hill's race-lap record there and get within the same second as Behra. But I didn't know any of this at the time. Nobody gave me any signals, so I had no idea how I was doing. Back at the pits I was told nothing. They simply changed two front wheels and sent me out again.' The new wheels were larger; Dan was cautioned to proceed with care.

After a lap or two Gurney reached his usual braking point before the fast right-hand Parabolica – only to have the front wheels lock. After an attempt to unlock them, he recalled, 'I was way past any shut-off point, so I was headed for the bank outside the turn. I hit that going semi-backwards and the Ferrari flipped up in the air, threw me virtually out and then stuffed me back in. I had grass all up and down my back. It righted on its wheels – right side up. This new, young American driver had just crashed the fastest Formula 1 car that Ferrari had ever built shortly after Jean Behra had set a new lap record with it. So I figured I was doing a very good job!

'They asked me what went wrong. I said, "I thought I was being careful enough but there was nothing wrong with the car. It was my fault. You warned me. I acknowledged the warning and I went ahead. I made a mistake." I think that really touched old Enzo. He was used to guys coming in and blaming the cars. So – strange as it may seem – three weeks later I was driving my first Grand Prix race.'

Reims in the French champagne country was the venue for his Formula 1 debut and the date of the race was 5 July 1959. 'Team manager Romolo Tavoni told me, "We have four cars at Reims, and one is yours.' I had no other testing after that Monza test and before that race, no anything. I didn't know what to expect. All I knew was: ready or not, here we come!' In fact Ferrari took five cars to Reims, which, as the combined French Grand Prix and GP d'Europe, offered one of the season's richest purses. Fortunately for Dan it was one of the circuits on which he had raced the previous summer.

Dan qualified 12th in his V-6 Ferrari Dino, about 2 seconds off the front-row times. He did this, wrote Denis Jenkinson, 'with effortless ease.' Although this was the insouciant impression that Dan successful projected, then and throughout his racing career, the actual situation in the cockpit was somewhat different, as the driver told Steve McNamara: 'Boy, is it dangerous! Reims is flat and it's marked out with hay bales – but try hitting a hay bale at 160. Those high-speed bends are really something. I wasn't prepared for that sort of thing and I don't like them particularly. Did I have trouble putting my foot down? You said it. You have to figure whether you're being brave or just being foolish.'

Practice days had been hot but the race day was sizzling, reaching 110°F. Under a blazing sun the road surface was starting to break up, as the drivers found on a few pre-race laps. Always chaotic, the start at Reims

was even more so for Gurney, who from his fifth-row grid position had to dodge the stalled Ferrari of Behra in the second row. Fastest qualifier Tony Brooks's Ferrari roared into a lead it would never lose. Gurney found himself in a mid-field battle with Bruce McLaren's Cooper and team-mate Olivier Gendebien, among others.

'The race itself was anticlimactic,' Dan said. 'It didn't last all that long for me, only 20 of the 50 laps. I was knocked out with a stone through the radiator thrown up by Graham Hill's Lotus.' Nevertheless he did get up to fifth at one point and was sixth when he retired. 'When I looked the car over back in the pits it was a sorry sight,' Gurney told Bill Nolan. 'The engine was smoking, the windscreen was cracked in three places and the entire body was pitted with numerous stone holes. I was disappointed not to finish, but relieved to be out of the hailstorm.' This, and a DNF at Le Mans, would be Dan's only retirements in nine starts for the works Ferrari team in 1959.

Meanwhile the Machiavellian internal politicking that so often flourished in the Ferrari team was taking its toll on the fiery Jean Behra. The newcomer became a lightning rod for Ferrari's anti-Behra faction. 'Through no fault of his own,' wrote Denis Jenkinson, at Ferrari Dan 'began to drive as fast as Behra. Both on sports cars and Grand Prix cars Behra was finding that Gurney was close on his heels, and this gave the people at Ferrari who were not pro-Behra an opportunity to make unnecessary remarks in loud voices.'

'Behra had never been happy with us,' Phil Hill recalled. 'He resented Brooks as a Number One, was uncomfortable at the performance of a newcomer like Dan Gurney, complained about always being given the slowest car – which was simply not true – and lost his temper more often than the Italians, which is going some!' Some of the most lurid blow-ups occurred at Reims over the assignment of cars. The upshot was that Jean Behra and Ferrari parted company that July, leaving a gap in Maranello's customary three-car Formula 1 line-up.

Who would fill that gap? Briton Cliff Allison was on the Ferrari strength; he and Gurney had become close friends. Olivier Gendebien had finished a worthy fourth for Ferrari at Reims. But over and above these two Enzo Ferrari chose Dan Gurney to complete his Grand Prix threesome. 'I think he sensed that there was something there,' Dan reflected. This was confirmed by Ferrari in *Piloti, che gente...* in which he remembered Gurney 'as strong, down-to-earth and serious' and referred to him in almost affectionate terms as his 'talented and courageous "Marine".'

His decision was fully justified by Dan's performance in the season's last three races. He qualified third and placed second at Berlin's high-speed Avus track where, Phil Hill recalled, 'Dan seemed to take to this banked type of high-speed competition.' Most convincing was his performance at Monsanto Park in Lisbon. 'The circuit was a genuine road course which tended to sort out the men from the boys,' reported *Autosport*. Of Gurney's third place it wrote, 'The young American certainly drove well and kept the red cars in the picture.'

Dan finished the Formula 1 season with a fourth in the Italian GP at Monza. 'Dan Gurney really showed his mettle,' praised *Autosport*. 'The American was cool, calm and collected, and did well to hold off the experienced Trintignant for more than half the race.' Later the British weekly wrote: 'Dan Gurney is undoubtedly the find of the season. Almost unknown until this year, the young American has proved that he can hold his own with the best European drivers.'

One post-season summary read in part as follows: 'Dan Gurney ranks as one of the Grand Prix discoveries of 1959... He may, as has been reported, consider himself a potential World Champion, but there is no visible arrogance in him, nor any mock modesty either. Dan Gurney seems to me to be a very natural talented phenomenon.'

This was the trenchant assessment of Louis Stanley, brother-in-law of the owner of the BRM team for which Dan signed to drive in 1960. Although some aspects of his future at Ferrari had been unclear – and Dan would later regret not having clarified them personally with Enzo Ferrari – one was not: the Italian's reluctance to succumb to the need to build one of those ugly rear-engined cars. In the race at Lisbon, said Dan, 'I had a front-row seat for the design contest. I could see that an

engine in the rear, behind the driver, was the way to go.' And BRM was building a car like that for 1960.

Talent-spotter John Wyer at Aston Martin was keen to engage Dan and offered a package of £5,000 ($14,000) to retain him for both GP racing and sports cars, but Aston's Grand Prix car was front-engined – not the wave of the future. BRM agreed to match this amount and leave Dan free for sports cars and other categories. The deal was done in November for a three-year period. 'I think we are very fortunate to have signed him,' wrote BRM engineer Peter Berthon, 'as he is the only young driver with the long-term potential of a Stirling Moss.'

Dan raced for BRM for only one year after receiving what he called 'a rude awakening.' Innocently, he had assumed after his Ferrari season that top-ranked racing cars were reliable: 'Those Ferraris were like anvils. You could just whale on them and not feel concerned about them coming apart.'

At BRM, however, 'It was essentially the opposite of the Ferrari season. There were quite a few instances where their stuff just fell apart. Jo Bonnier, Graham Hill and I were team-mates and combined we had 27 starts – more or less nine each – and three finishes out of the 27 starts. We each had a finish. One. I liked the people. I liked the mechanics. We just couldn't keep it together.'

Worse, one failure caused a horrendous crash at Zandvoort in the Dutch GP. The pipe to the BRM's single inboard rear disc brake failed approaching a hairpin at the end of a 160mph straight and Dan was launched by a sand dune at high speed through an advertising sign, into the air and across a spectator pathway, killing an 18-year-old youth. Wrote Raymond Mays, 'All of us who had seen the car flung in the air were convinced that Dan could not possibly have survived.' A shocked Gurney suffered bruising, a cracked wrist and cuts from a barbed-wire fence; he still has the scars.

Between that crash and his many retirements 'BRM caused me to lose my faith in engineers,' Dan reflected. The Zandvoort incident also affected his braking: 'I was plenty hungry and was going into corners as deep as anyone. I don't think I've ever regained the ability I had then to really get the most out of the brakes. I never made quite the same commitment after that.' Instead he concentrated on *not* braking unnecessarily, a technique that his later Indy driving refined.

Not braking was just what the next Grand Prix Formula 1 required, with its 1½-litre engines from 1961. Dan, a big man who had made his name in big cars, was not a fan of the new Formula. He likened driving its cars to pushing hard in a VW Beetle, keeping pedal to metal while rowing along with the gear lever: 'They were so underpowered that you reset your hourglass and started going up through the gears.'

Dan warmed up for the new Formula in 1960 with some drives in a 1½-litre Lotus 18-Climax entered by Louise Bryden-Brown, who had loaned him her Denzel in California four years earlier. He had a great race with it at Brands Hatch in August, taking pole ahead of Clark in a similar car and Moss's Porsche. Through the race he, Clark and Surtees had a ding-dong battle that Clark finally won by two-fifths of a second. Gurney set a new Formula 2 record on his final lap.

In July Dan raced a works Porsche single-seater at the Solitude circuit near Stuttgart, a hairy 7-mile road course through forested countryside. As a getting-to-know-Porsche exercise this was highly successful, with Dan finishing fifth after an exciting and hard-fought race. 'I've never had to drive so hard in my life just for fifth place,' he said afterward.

In 1961 Gurney signed to pilot Porsches, looking forward to a long stay with the already-famous German company. He had driven for them for more than a year when, in July 1962, he met the beautiful dark-haired Evi Butz, assistant to Porsche racing director and PR chief Huschke von Hanstein. Their relationship, warm and mutual, remained their secret until the late summer of 1968 when Evi surprised her colleagues by telling them that she was leaving her Porsche post to go to America to tie the knot with Gurney, then finalising his divorce. They married in Las Vegas on 7 July 1969 and have two sons of their own, Justin and Alexander.

His two seasons with Porsche – 1961 and '62 – were fulfilling for Dan Gurney, he told Tim Considine: 'That's when I learned how to drive. It's difficult to learn anything if your car keeps breaking down all the time. You need more time to get a feeling for what's going to happen so you don't make the sorts of silly mistakes

that a young charger wants to make. With Porsche, here was a platform that just would hang in there. It wasn't terribly quick, but it was quick enough to always be a threat.'

After a gearbox problem in a pre-season event Dan had a trouble-free 1961. He tied with Stirling Moss for third in world championship points behind Phil Hill and the late Wolfgang von Trips. His best finishes were second in the Italian and American GPs and also at Reims after a fantastic slipstreaming battle with winner Giancarlo Baghetti's Ferrari.

Equipped with Porsche's new flat-eight engine, Gurney finally scored his first Formula 1 victory in 1962 at Rouen in July. 'It was very rough at Rouen, just shook the devil out of the cars, the steering, the gear train and everything.' Dan's Porsche survived the battering that other cars didn't and the race came to him: 'There wasn't anything spectacular about inheriting a race. It wasn't terribly thrilling from my own standpoint because I wasn't really battling after Brabham dropped out. Nevertheless, I was really happy – even though I had a nice case of the flu that day – and the Porsche people were really happy too.' Particularly happy were the wives and girlfriends of the mechanics, who had vowed not to shave until Porsche won a Grand Prix.

The next weekend Dan raced and won again in a non-championship race at Solitude, making a lot more Germans very happy. 'Solitude was the biggest crowd I'd ever seen outside of Indy,' Dan said, recalling his victory lap after the race: 'They said it was around 350,000. A car from Stuttgart won it, so guys were all throwing their hats in the air. The sea of hats that were in the air as we drove around went like a wave. Hats were even coming out of the forest. It was sensational.

'Those were great years,' Dan recalled. 'Porsche was not "Teutonic efficiency" and all that, not at all. They were hard-working with good camaraderie, had senses of humour and just kept going. I still cherish my days with the Porsche team.' But those days came to an end: 'Unfortunately Porsche decided to pack it in at the end of the season. It was a great shame. It might have been the right thing for them but it left me hunting around.'

Gurney resolved to look for a team where he could

enjoy some stability. He felt he had 'singed' his bridges at BRM and Ferrari. Lotus was a possibility. He admired the way Lotus racers sacrificed everything for speed. But he wasn't comfortable with the fragility of Colin Chapman's cars: 'They pay the price for speed in teams of structural integrity. On paper they're strong enough, but in the field they have a history of more failures than the others.'

Two-time world champion Jack Brabham was his choice, Dan told Barrie Gill: 'Jack was just beginning. I had seen his first car racing at Watkins Glen and I was very impressed. It was a nice clean little car that looked as good as anything out there. So that seemed as though it was pretty good way to go. I went to Jack and talked to him. He thought he could work out something. There were no guarantees that we would be successful.'

One man who thought they might do well was Stirling Moss, as he confided to Ken Purdy: 'Dan Gurney is going to drive for Jack Brabham this year and that is not the worst idea Jack ever had. I consider Gurney to be, right now, one of the best drivers in the world and one of the fastest. Gurney is competitive. He's a man who will have a go. He won't say: "The car isn't much good and I won't bother." He'll go. A very nice man, too. He looks exactly what he is, one of the few human beings I know who does.'

This was, wrote Brabham, 'the first time I had taken on a "name" driver to join me in Formula 1. Dan was a driver I admired a lot – so much, in fact, that I almost decided to retire from the driving side and leave Dan to carry on, with myself directing operations from the pits. During 1963, however, the great things we expected from our efforts did not quite materialise. Twice Dan retired when he was holding a certain second place in a championship race. He finished second in two other races, and I achieved one second place.'

Dan was generous about the Brabham team's ragged reliability record: 'We felt that we had a little bad luck. Unfortunately our troubles seemed to come in a race and not in practice. In 1964 we had the lead in about eight of the Grand Prix races before something or other went wrong.' Nevertheless, said Brabham, 'in 1964 he won the French Grand Prix at Rouen and the Mexican Grand Prix at the end of the season. We felt that our Formula 1 car was just on the verge of really good things.'

Finance was one constraint, Dan said: 'It was kind of hand to mouth then, very austere. Jack was always pretty careful with the money.' This was confirmed to Mike Lawrence by designer Ron Tauranac: 'Jack ran a tight ship, so there was only one mechanic on each car. I think that one extra mechanic on the team might have made the difference; it would have been a case of laying out a little more and gaining a bigger return.' The best return that Dan could eke from his 1965 season was three third places plus seconds in the final two races in America and Mexico.

A new GP Formula was on the cards for 1966, a doubling of engine capacity to 3 litres. Brabham hoped to retain Gurney for what promised to be a rewarding return to real horsepower: 'I thought if we could get Dan to go on driving for us in 1966 I would retire and spend more time on the preparation of the cars and see that they were right for Dan. Then Dan decided to go off on his own and build his Eagles.'

'I didn't want to leave Jack,' Dan explained. 'It's just that the opportunity to start my own team came along at that time. And that was something I really wanted to do.' A lifelong dream was within his grasp. 'Grand Prix racing included that Olympic element,' he added. 'You were racing on behalf of your country, and that always meant a little bit extra to me. I am very proud of being an American and as a driver it is quite meaningful to me that after each race they play the National Anthem of the country the winner is from.' He would invest all – and more – in an effort to win with an American car.

David Phipps thoughtfully chooses an almost identical position at Rouen for the French Grand Prix finishes in 1962 (opposite top) and 1964 (opposite). In these races Dan Gurney scores the first-ever championship Formula 1 victories for Porsche and Brabham respectively.

In spite of a testing accident that leaves the tail of his Grand Prix Ferrari severely crumpled, Dan is given a chance to drive one in a Grand Prix at Reims on 5 July 1959. There he takes a breather on the roadway and settles into the car with Enzo Ferrari's close collaborator Luigi Bazzi behind him. In the Portuguese GP he trashes his Ferrari's nose but finishes best Ferrari in third.

After his Ferrari Formula 1 debut at Reims (above) in which he retires, Gurney drives to an excellent second place behind Tony Brooks at Berlin's Avus Track, where he is snapped on the high banking. Tragically his friend and former Ferrari team-mate Jean Behra is killed at the same race meeting.

Seen racing at Monaco (left) and Reims (above), Dan Gurney likes the British BRM car and team but is let down by chronic unreliability that destroys his confidence in engineers. A rear-brake failure at Zandvoort causes one of the severest crashes of his career. Dan is helped by jacket-wearing fellow driver Roy Salvadori, who walks the bandaged American back to the pits.

Although the tall Gurney judges that the new 1½-litre formula of 1961 is 'just what he doesn't need', he finds a safe haven with Porsche and its well-built cars. Brussels (above) in April is his only retirement in '61. At the Nürburgring (below), where Dan starts and finishes seventh, he is outside right. Brabham, leading, is followed by Stirling Moss, Jo Bonnier and Phil Hill.

In the 1961 Grand Prix of Monaco Dan finishes fifth, two laps behind winner Stirling Moss. He is being caught up by the Ferrari of fellow Californian Phil Hill (38). During practice at the Station Hairpin Dan mugs for friends – as if at the wheel of a kiddie car – and later tackles the corner in a much more serious frame of mind.

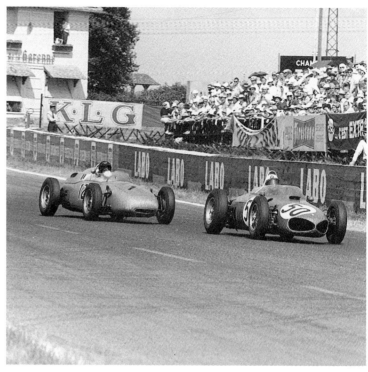

The Reims tradition for slipstreaming duels is spectacularly upheld on 2 July 1961 in the battle between eventual winner Giancarlo Baghetti in a Ferrari and Dan Gurney's Porsche (12) with intervention from Jo Bonnier (10). The Ferrari's narrow victory is unavoidable, as Gurney explains: 'I tried half a dozen times to find out what was the best of the options I had. I could

either come out of the last turn behind him and draught by – but not before the start-finish line – or come out ahead of him, and he could get by me before the start-finish line. Now, I could easily have been first out of the last turn and then blocked him. But we didn't do that. It wasn't that that sort of thing didn't cross your mind, but you felt almost honour-bound not to do it.'

In 1962 Dan Gurney scores Porsche's only championship Grand Prix success at Rouen on 8 July (previous spread and lower right). He finishes a frustrated third in a wet German Grand Prix (above right with Graham Hill's BRM). He critiques the new flat-8 Formula 1 Porsche in its first appearance at Zandvoort in May (left, top and bottom). Ferry Porsche is in trilby and raincoat, engineer Helmuth Bott in leather jacket and Jo Bonnier in white helmet. Huschke von Hanstein is at the front of the car with Bernard Cahier at the left.

Gurney and Jack Brabham share a laugh at Watkins Glen in 1965 where Dan finishes second. For the Monaco GP in 1964 mechanic Tim Wall converts Dan's suit to shorts to aid race-cooling. At Mexico City in 1964 Gurney squirts fuel into the injector stacks of his Brabham BT7 for the pre-race warm-up. He drives through to victory.

The Gurney-Clark rivalry is in full swing at the 1965 Dutch Grand Prix (above). Jimmy (6) wins while Dan (16) must settle for third behind Jackie Stewart. Dan is second at the same race in 1963 (below), where he gives a cheery wave to David Phipps.

Dan's two Brabham victories in 1964 are at Rouen (above) and Mexico City (below). In both races he starts second on the grid in a season in which he scores two pole positions. Dan is third-fastest qualifier at the Nürburgring (overleaf) where he leaps off the line ahead of Clark and the Ferrari of winner John Surtees (7). Dan pits twice for overheating problems and finishes tenth.

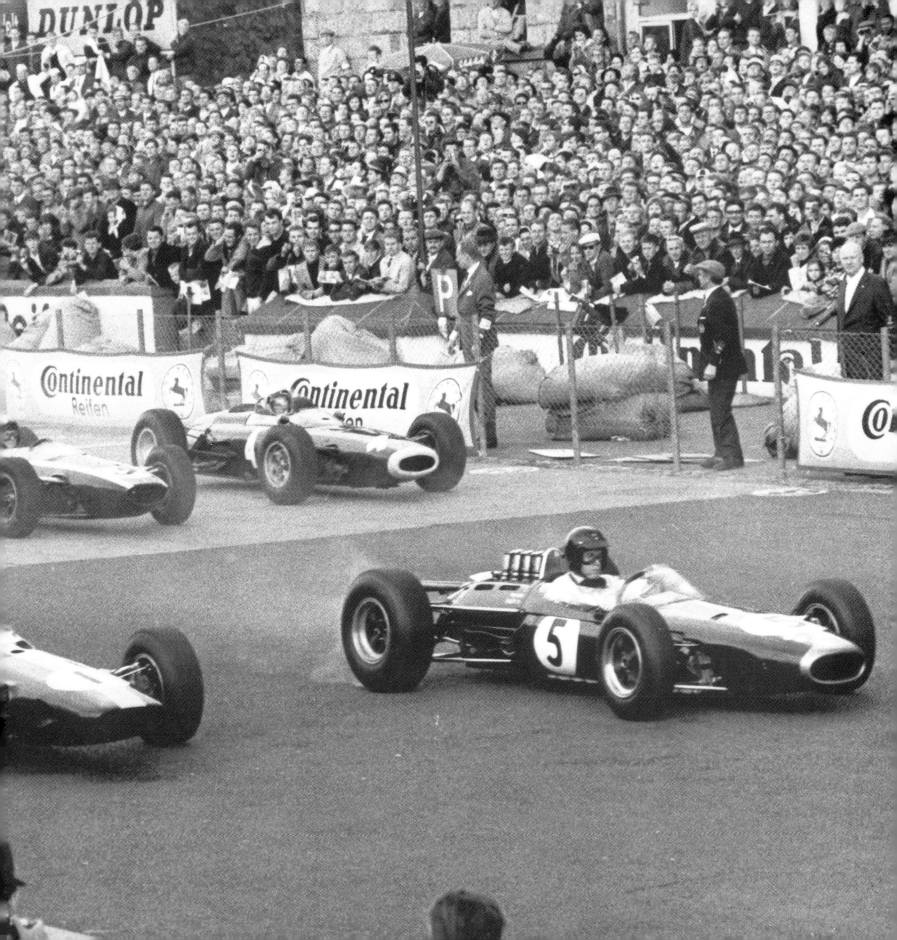

David Phipps catches Gurney correcting a slide at Silverstone in the 1963 British Grand Prix meeting. He qualifies second quickest but retires with engine failure. His uncharacteristic look is the result of borrowing a pair of Jack Brabham's goggles. The senior Rodriguez is among the first to greet the victorious Gurney (opposite) at the finish of the 1964 Mexican Grand Prix on 25 October. Dan's fine win is overshadowed by the drama surrounding the championship success of John Surtees.

CHAPTER 4

Iconoclasts at Indy

For the second year in a row a Grand Prix driver had come to Indy. The first in the modern era was Aussie Jack Brabham in 1961. The second, in 1962, was one of the drivers for Germany's Porsche team. But he wasn't one of the feared and detested Europeans, come to deprive the native sons of their Indy lucre. He was an American, indeed an American who had in his youth been a fan of oval-track racing. Yet Dan Gurney had taken an entirely different path to America's richest and most famous race. Instead of the midget and sprint-car ladders that most Indy drivers climbed to fame, Dan arrived at Indianapolis, Indiana, through sports and Grand Prix cars. And what began as a fascination morphed into a mania.

As an American racing driver Dan was assumed abroad to be an Indy intimate. 'Wherever I'd go,' he said, 'even in Europe, people would ask me if I had driven the Indianapolis 500. Before I'd even seen it, it

It's not a victory but Dan can be — and is – very happy with his second-place finish in the 1968 Indianapolis 500-mile race. In his five previous Indy starts he finished seventh, was withdrawn once, crashed once and retired twice.

became an obsession to me to run in it. And once I'd seen it, it became an obsession to me to win it.'

Gurney first saw Indianapolis-type cars in his first year in Europe, 1958. They came to him, for a race on Monza's banked oval track. With their solid axles and rumbustious four-cylinder Offy engines, the 'roadsters' were not, Dan realised, at the cutting edge of racing technology. He enjoyed meeting their drivers, however, especially 1952 Indy winner Troy Ruttman. With Troy and his wife in a borrowed Renault Dauphine he drove from race to race that summer, soaking up Indy lore along the way.

By 1961 Dan was able to start making plans to race at Indy in '62. 'I have no idea what'll happen at the Speedway,' he told Joe Scalzo. 'I've never even seen the track – but I really want to give 'er a try.' He made his debut there with the help and support of two Speedway iconoclasts, one successful and the other less so.

Iconoclast Mark I was Texas oilman John 'Jack' Zink. After winning Indy with a Kurtis in 1955 Zink was the first to commission a complete car from A. J. Watson, who went on to become one of Indy's most successful car builders. He brought Zink another win in 1956.

Now the Texan had a radical new car for 1962. It was not only rear-engined but also turbine-powercd. And Dan Gurney had agreed to try to qualify it.

Needing to slot his Indy commitment between his European races, Dan was on the Speedway for the first day of practice, 28 April. He learned the track in a Watson-built roadster from the Zink stable and by the next day was able to breeze through all the phases of the mandatory 'driver's test' that required set numbers of laps to be driven at progressively higher speeds with smoothness and consistency. Trackside experts couldn't recall any Speedway rookie successfully passing his test any earlier or more easily.

After a detour to Sicily to compete in the Targa Florio, Dan was back in Indiana the following week to take his first laps in the turbine-powered Zink 'Trackburner'. Watching his efforts closely was Iconoclast Mark II, Californian Mickey Thompson. Better known as a hot-rodder who had successfully attacked international speed records, the ebullient Thompson was also making his Speedway debut with neat rear-engined cars powered by modified Buick V-8s, their tubular space frames designed by Briton John Crosthwaite.

'I arranged with Gurney that if neither of [Zink's] cars qualified, he would drive for me,' Thompson told Griff Borgeson. 'The old heads called me a fool for choosing a driver without a shred of Speedway experience.' The Speedway novice was extracting some speed from the Boeing-powered Zink; 142.5mph was not too bad compared to fastest laps around 149. But its chances of qualifying for the race were nil. Dan took up Mickey Thompson's offer.

Gurney, said Thompson, 'analysed the chassis as only a highly intelligent driver with his specialised experience could. He dictated change after change in its adjustments and each one made for quicker lap times. Finally he told Crosthwaite, "Now it's perfect. Do not lay a wrench on this car. Is that clear?" He gave the impression that he'd break the neck of anyone who tampered with the combination that he had developed.'

Of the three Thompson entries Dan's was the only one to qualify, an impressive eighth fastest at an average of 147.9mph for four laps of the 2½-mile four-cornered

track. In the race Gurney was able to stay within the top ten even though, as he recalled, the modified Buick 'never ran right from the beginning. It was detonating and surging severely. In fact it seldom felt as though it ran on all eight cylinders.' This, thought Dan, was probably responsible for the failure of its transaxle after 94 of the 200 laps.

Disappointing though his outing was, Dan had really taken to Indy. His experience on the dauntingly fast European tracks had prepared him well for the Speedway. 'Indianapolis is very much akin to other forms of racing,' he told Peter Manso. 'I think it's easier to make the transition from Grand Prix racing to Indianapolis than it is from Indianapolis to Grand Prix racing or from, say, quarter-mile or mile ovals to Indianapolis.' Certainly the graduates of the latter school seemed disproportionately represented among those smiting the walls with regularity.

'There's more to it than just turning left,' Dan continued. 'It's a contest with cars and drivers, human beings, and in theory all have to do the same things. Therefore it's just as easy or just as difficult for everyone. So to win it you not only have to turn left but you have to turn left better than the rest of them. So while it may be simpler, it's certainly not any less difficult.' Clearly Indy had attracted another acolyte.

Between qualifying and racing at Indy Dan brought his air ticket bill for the month to $3,000 by fitting in two other European races, the 'Ring 1,000 Kilometres and the Dutch Grand Prix at Zandvoort. At the latter race Colin Chapman unveiled his new Lotus 25, which introduced full-monocoque frame structure to Formula 1. Stepping out of his tube-framed Porsche, Gurney was stunned by the rational simplicity of the Lotus. Thinking of his recent Indiana experiences he said to Chapman, 'My God, you know if someone took a car like this to Indianapolis they could win with it.'

After the Grand Prix this thought refused to fade away. Dan contacted Chapman and said, 'Would you like to come to Indy to see what it's like?' The famed designer, respected as a successful innovator and resourceful entrepreneur, had never been to America's greatest race. He was persuaded by Dan's offer of a flight ticket to make the long trek to the '62 500. It was an invitation that proved historic.

With his penchant for original thinking in auto design Colin Chapman qualified as Iconoclast Mark III in Dan's first year at the Speedway. Later, wrote Chapman intimate Gerard Crombac, 'when he described the old-fashioned front-engined "roadsters" he had seen, he was laughing his head off!' But he wasn't laughing about the Indy prize money, which for 1962 winner Rodger Ward was $125,015.

It would have been easy enough to build a car to take the veteran Offy engine, but neither Dan nor Colin favoured this solution. Dan's pace with the Buick V-8 in '62 suggested that a stock-block engine could do the job, even though at that time it was given no displacement advantage. Similar thoughts had been brewing in the mind of Ford executive Don Frey, who'd also been at Indy in 1962. Ford was in the early months of its 'Total Performance' campaign and Indy was next on its agenda.

Earlier in the year Gurney had met many of the key Ford decision-makers at Daytona, Florida. There he'd been invited to drive a Ford stock car in the Daytona 500. Although his engine had failed in the race he had impressed the Ford people with his speed and commitment in what was for him a completely new form of racing. For Chapman as well Ford was *terra cognita*, thanks to his work with them on the Lotus Cortina. The conspirators selected Ford as their target.

The British Grand Prix was held at Aintree on 21 July, a Saturday. Dan placed ninth for Porsche and Jim Clark won for Lotus. Then Chapman and Gurney flew to America. On the Monday, 23 July, they were at Ford's Detroit 'glass house' headquarters with outline plans for an Indy attack. Few sponsorship pitches in the long history of motor racing have been more enthusiastically and positively welcomed.

That same week plans were put in motion to build Ford-powered Lotuses for Indy. The package was compelling: an outstanding chassis builder and two fine drivers. Clark was then only one point behind Graham Hill in the chase for the Formula 1 World Championship and Gurney – who was on the team as a reward for his role as a catalyst in the project – was a vital American ingredient. And the reward was of more than token

value, Dan said: 'On that deal alone I made 180 grand which was pretty good for the time – although the tax rate was probably in the low 70 per cent.'

The pay was good but Dan earned it. He was the Stateside driving talent for the extensive testing that Ford invested in the development of its engine. He was at the wheel for the tests at the Speedway at the end of March 1963 that confirmed the competitiveness of the Lotus-Ford with a lap at 150.5mph – second fastest in the Speedway's history. That set the seal on Ford's Indy plans and led to the final contracts and the entries for the race.

His Lotus races on oval tracks were anticlimactic for Dan. In '63 he touched the unforgiving Indy wall during practice on the first day of qualifications and had to race the back-up car, which he brought home seventh. Later in the season he joined Clark in the front row for the Trenton 200 but retired when his oil scavenge pump's entry was blocked by a piece of piston skirt. In the 1964 Indy 500, powered by new four-cam Ford engines, the Lotuses suffered 'chunking' problems with their too-soft special Dunlop tyres – bits were flying off. When a tyre tread of Clark's Lotus came adrift while he was leading, tilting him into the wall, Chapman elected to withdraw Gurney, who was well back after a long early pit stop to attend to a balky fuel-selector valve.

These were two frustrating years for the man who had inspired the Lotus-Ford Indy project. Dan had great respect for the abilities of Colin Chapman. 'He was a racer to the core,' he said to Alan Henry. 'When you were part of his team you quickly came to realise that this was a guy working at redefining the cutting edge of racing technology. That was a real motivating factor, believe me.' But Chapman's controversial choice of the unproven Dunlops in 1964 had been a redefinition too far for Gurney.

Also niggling was that the 'furrin' Lotus-Ford effort, backed so heavily by Ford, was deeply resented by the Indy establishment, which naturally associated Gurney with it. For a patriot like Dan this was discomfiting. And Dan knew that the relationship between Clark and Chapman was so close that he could never hope to gain an advantage over the Scots driver as long as he stayed with the Lotus set-up.

Ironically Chapman's decision to fit smaller 15-inch wheels to his 1963 Indy racers led to the creation of the Eagles that became one of his strongest rivals. When the other teams demanded to be allocated some of the tyres that Firestone (then Indy's sole supplier) had made exclusively for Lotus, the tyre firm was unable to comply. The unlucky teams were at once on the phone to Firestone's great Akron rival, Goodyear, which had been progressively moving into motor sports. 'Come to Indy,' they pleaded, 'and we'll use your tyres.'

Both alert to the opportunity this presented and well connected at Goodyear, Carroll Shelby laid plans of his own. During a London taxi ride late in 1962 Carroll had learned that Dan Gurney had begun thinking his own thoughts about building racing cars in America. If Goodyear was to make an impact at the Speedway it would need an association with capable, progressive teams – of which there were few. Having been close to Lotus, Gurney had a good grasp of the facilities and personnel that were needed. He also liked the style of Lotus chief designer Len Terry.

In the meantime, Dan had put his Ford-Lotus largesse to good use by setting up a small racing team of his own in 1964. With this as background, he and Shelby took the case for the establishment of a new racing team to Goodyear. Their credentials were impeccable; the reception was warm. With a deal agreed, the participants marched into the office of Goodyear's president for a blessing from the top.

'What are you planning to call it?' he asked. Before Dan had a chance to reply he added, 'How about All American Racers?'

The Goodyear man was thinking of other sports, such as American college football, in which a 'dream team' is nominated from the best the nation has to offer. The Shelby-Gurney effort could be seen as just such an 'all American' effort in the racing field. Although, Dan said, 'it didn't appeal to me at the time, it was done in such a way that we felt obligated to say, "Yes, that's a great name and that's what it will be."'

The newly baptised AAR first attacked Indy in 1965. Still as part of the Ford deal with Lotus, Dan received a brand-new and improved Lotus-Ford which he raced as his own entry. A great motorcycle enthusiast, Dan

organised sponsorship from Yamaha. This conferred the boon of kimono-style turquoise and black outfits for the crew that won them a special award for the best-dressed team.

That year finally brought a Lotus Indy victory, but not for Dan. Qualifying superbly on the outside of the front row, he was battling for second with Parnelli Jones when his engine expired just past the 100-mile mark. Gurney was one of three users of the four-cam Ford to retire. 'Part of the cam gear drive had somehow missed the heat-treat (hardening) operation,' wrote Leo Levine. 'Gurney, the man who was the catalyst in the programme, was also the man who through coincidence got the short end.' Later in the season Dan qualified and finished third at Milwaukee in this car.

After Indy in 1965 Len Terry left Lotus to design the new AAR racing cars. An early plan had been to call the Indy cars 'Gurneys' and the AAR Grand Prix cars 'Eagles', but finally 'Eagle' was chosen for both. The Gurney contribution was immortalised in the letter 'G' that embraced an eagle's head in the handsome emblem designed by Dan's father. By September the new AAR facility at Santa Ana was open and ready to start building six cars for the '66 race.

Goodyear backing or no, Dan Gurney had taken on a huge responsibility in setting up and running AAR. Carroll Shelby would not be involved for long. Carroll, Dan told *Autoweek*, 'had his own agendas. Carroll was more going at it to make money. We knew it was going to be a lot of work, and to be honest, Carroll didn't want to do all of that work and not get paid. I don't blame him. I was more of a fan. Racing's always been a labour of love with me.' By 1967 Shelby would be divorced from AAR, his interest acquired by Dan.

On the positive side, having his own cars and team was hugely liberating for Dan. Hitherto he had been at the mercy of the design skills and the preparation standards of others. With good reason, Gurney felt that he had much to contribute to a successful effort outside as well as inside the cockpit. 'We can make our own mistakes with these cars,' he explained to Alan Henry. 'We have no one to blame, good or bad, but ourselves, and that's fine with me.' The buck stopped at Dan's big new desk in the 16,000-square-foot AAR building.

Sunday 13 March 1966 was a big day for Gurney and his crew. He drove a beak-nosed Eagle in anger for the first time, running counter-clockwise at Riverside because the engine's oil reservoir and other features of the chassis were designed for left-hand turns. In his 35 test laps the cornering was good but the car's weaving on the straight 'gave me grey hairs'. An argument over the suspension geometry did little to improve relations between Dan and designer Terry. The Briton would leave AAR in September.

Five Eagles were ready for Indy and to AAR's great credit all five made the race even though speeds were much higher in 1966, thanks to the tyre improvements encouraged by the Firestone-Goodyear competition. Dan had a fraught qualifying. On the first day his three attempts were spoiled by clutch failure, ending any hope of a pole position; only first-day Indy qualifiers can claim that. A speed of 160.5mph on the second day was adequate but left Dan back on the seventh of the 11 starting rows.

Farther forward would have been better. As the cars crossed the line for the flying start a multiple pile-up developed in mid-field before they reached the first turn. When the dust settled Dan ruefully observed his car's complete lack of wheels on its left-hand side. He was scathing in his contempt: 'Why 33 of the world's top racing drivers find it impossible to drive down a straight piece of track without running into each other sure beats the hell out of me.'

Dan was shaken but unhurt. Nevertheless the chaotic crash did nothing to encourage his wife Arleo to think more highly of his job description. 'I don't like Indy,' she told Bill Libby. 'I don't see the purpose of it – round and round in a circle. It's all brute strength and speed. It's too dangerous; frightening. Oh, I do see the purpose of it: money. It's not enough. It's not worth it to me. I know Dan could be killed.' Pressurised by Dan's high-risk career, their relationship was deteriorating.

Safety had a high priority for Gurney. He was the first to wear a full-face helmet and, later, the Nomex balaclava that added valuable fire protection. 'The first driver to wear such a thing was Dan Gurney,' said mechanic Clint Brawner. 'I remember Dan always acted a little embarrassed when he pulled the hood on, as if someone would think of him as being less of a "he-man" for wearing one.' Precisely because he was obviously all man, Gurney was a role model for safety advances.

Before the 1967 500 Dan reflected on his Indy attempts to Bill Libby: 'Every year this damn place beats me black and blue and I feel like giving it up, and every year I come back bigger and better than ever. If I lose a few more years, I'm liable to build enough cars to fill the field by myself, then one of my cars will have to win. I can't be the first Grand Prix driver to win this thing any more. I can't be the first in a rear-engine car any more. But I can still win it. And I can at least run more than 20 yards, like I did last year, and half of that on my belly.'

Gurney said he was well aware of the impact of his career on his family: 'People don't realise that racing drivers are like other people. They have families who worry about them and who they worry about.' But he admitted that he was hooked: 'Indy is like a magnet to me. So is racing. I've had so much frustration, so much failure, so little luck in racing and at Indy. I should have given it up long ago. But I love it so. Maybe my luck will turn.'

In 1967, as we learned in Chapter 1, it didn't turn. That November, however, Dan scored his first personal USAC race victory in an Eagle. He led from pole to finish in the Rex Mays 300 at Riverside, taking special pride in winning a race named for one of America's greatest drivers. He would win the same race in the same way the following year and score a victory at Canada's Mosport road course as well, also from pole.

Shrugging off competition from turbine-powered Lotuses, Eagles flew at Indy in 1968. Dan placed second in a car powered by a Ford V-8 with his own Gurney-Weslake cylinder heads, on the same lap as winner Bobby Unser, also Eagle-mounted. Now a bona fide member of the Indy establishment, Gurney was decidedly anti the revolution represented by turbine engines: 'I am certainly not against progress, but I strongly feel that automobile racing and piston engines are synonymous. They could probably construct a super-quality baseball that would go a lot further, for instance, but that would mean changing the entire sport and, after all, we're involved in an established sport, not a transportation industry. It ought to be up to the people to decide whether they want to listen to "vacuum cleaners" or highly developed piston engines, which to me is the essence of the sport. If we are going down at Indy, we are going down fighting.'

Gurney kept fighting with a stock-block engine in 1969 in a new car, dubbed the 'Santa Ana' after its home town. It was unveiled there on 25 April 1969, which was declared 'Dan Gurney Day' in Santa Ana. Although the new car delivered some frustrations in practice, it also delivered another second-place Indy finish for Dan. In USAC road races it scored victories for Gurney at Indianapolis Raceway Park and Sears Point.

Among several other podium positions for the Santa Ana was a third place at Seattle International Raceway in a race that had special significance for Dan: it was the Dan Gurney 200, named to honour his career and achievements. Its tribute to Gurney mentioned that he and Jim Clark were the only double winners of the Martini & Rossi Driver of the Year award, voted for by racing fans.

After a 1969 meeting at the Speedway a reconciliation with Len Terry led to a new Eagle for 1970. In its design Gurney requested the characteristics that he felt contributed to speed, which Mark Donohue described as follows: 'Dan's theories about making a car fast were: the lower the better, and soft springs give better road holding. Since speeds don't vary much at Indy, he put in very soft springs, jacked the car way up and let it sink down on the springs at speed. To prevent bottoming in the turns, he used very stiff anti-roll bars.'

In 1970 for the first time Dan chose a turbo-Offy to power his car. After his two second places in a row

Gurney was tipped to win, but the new chassis disappointed. From a fourth-row starting position Dan put in what he later called 'one of my better drives against the odds'. In spite of pitting no fewer than 11 times with handling and fuel problems he finished third in what was his final race at Indy.

Dan's last race at the wheel of an Eagle was at the opening event of the new Ontario Motor Speedway west of Riverside on 6 September 1970, America's Labor Day holiday. He was second-fastest qualifier at a sizzling 176.4mph and commanded the lead in the race, only to be delayed by a bungled pit stop. He fought back to third by half-distance of the 500-mile race but then was pitched into a wall by oil sprayed on a tyre by a broken oil line.

This was near the end of Dan's driving career, but not of AAR. With other drivers it would go on to many glories, not only in Indy cars but also in other series, including a dominant IMSA performance for Toyota. 'I have great faith in these people,' Gurney said of AAR in the 1990s, 'and it would have been awful to disband something that was capable of so much. I am proud of the fact that this team is like a large family, which most people want to stick with. That's why we've managed to keep coming back every time they say we're finished.

'I've been pretty good from the survival standpoint,' Gurney reflected recently, 'and I have a lot of technical curiosity combined with some aptitude. This business is not much fun unless you feel like you're on the cutting edge and have a very good chance of winning. It is sort of an extreme form of torture – mostly mental, but also physical. And I don't feel quite as old, especially when I am winning!'

Although Colin Chapman, Lotus and Ford are credited with starting the rear-engine revolution at Indy with Gurney as the catalyst, the highly professional private effort of Mickey Thompson in 1962 should not be overlooked. Gurney qualifies the Buick-powered tube-framed car very respectably but has to retire with final-drive problems aggravated by a rough-running engine.

Stanley Rosenthall follows Dan Gurney and Jim Clark to an unusual venue, the 1-mile oval at Trenton, New Jersey, for a 200-mile race on 22 September 1963. Gurney jokes with Clark and checks the time sheets with Colin Chapman. Dan looks the favourite for pole but is pipped by Clark; both are in the front row in their Lotus-Fords ahead of a swarm of front-engined 'roadsters'. Gurney is forced to retire by oil system failure in his pushrod Ford V-8.

Dan can afford to smile after engineering a deal between Lotus and Ford for Indianapolis that is lucrative for him personally. His luck is against him in the 1963 Indy 500, however. He crashes his race car (91) before qualifying and is obliged to race the back-up car (93). Gurney finishes seventh while team-mate Clark is second.

Gurney gains a measure of independence in the final year of his Lotus-Ford deal, 1965. Entered by his own team, his car is powered by Ford's new four-cam V-8. Dan warms up on sponsor Yamaha's motorcycle and qualifies a brilliant third quickest, winning the outside of the front row. Faulty timing gears stop him before quarter distance in the race.

Dan Gurney and his colleagues at All American Racers have every right to be proud of qualifying five of their Eagle-Fords at Indianapolis in 1966. Few handsomer cars have ever taken to that hallowed track. Dan's own Eagle Ford (previous spread and opposite) looks anything but pristine, however, after being caught up in a start-line crash. Gurney provides his views on the competence of his fellow drivers to ABC Television and looks about to perform a 'gotcha' on friend and rival Jim Clark.

In 1968 at Indy Dan Gurney gamely meets the demands of sponsors and press, also finding time for contemplation in the cockpit of his Eagle-Weslake. It is a good year for AAR with Bobby Unser winning in his Offy-powered Eagle and Dan placing second with his stock-block engine with Gurney-Weslake cylinder heads. Dan shares the success with ABC's Jim McKay (above) and sponsor Ozzie Olson (right). The car itself can scarcely be seen for the many decals of its supporters and sponsors (overleaf).

In 1969 at Indy Dan relies again on his Gurney-Weslake-Ford V-8 to power his new car, the 'Santa Ana', designed by Tony Southgate. Although it frustrates his search for ultimate speed the Santa Ana brings Gurney another strong second-place finish.

Briton Len Terry returns to the fold to design the 1970 Eagle for AAR. Dan chooses a turbocharged four-cylinder Offy to power his personal car, which he drives to a doughty third-place Indianapolis finish.

By 1970 Gurney, fed up with Ford, is affiliated with Plymouth as his suit badging indicates. He is interviewed for television after qualifying at 166.860mph with a crewman in the foreground holding the all-important tyre-temperature slip. Chief mechanic Wayne Leary stands over the cockpit as Dan suits up, and is chief pusher as the Eagle-Offy is returned to Gasoline Alley after 1970 qualifying. This symbolises Dan Gurney's final year at the Indianapolis Motor Speedway.

The pressures of racing at Indianapolis take a toll on a man. Dan Gurney progresses (across the top of the two pages) from 1962 to 1963, then 1965 with Bill Fowler and 1966 after his start-line crash. He matures (across the bottom) from 1967 to 1968, 1969 and, with Bobby Unser, 1970. After Dan steps down from driving Bobby is his chosen successor.

Dan Gurney's last Indy-car race is at California's Ontario Motor Speedway (overleaf left) on 6 September 1970. He qualifies at blistering speed and is among the leaders before he crashes out, spinning on his own oil, just before half distance. It's quite a contrast from the modest Mickey Thompson operation of 1962 (overleaf right) that first brings Dan Gurney to the start of an Indy-car event. The years between are marked by determination, creativity, perseverance and, above all, a search for ultimate speed.

With the track breaking up at Reims in July 1959 Dan Gurney is in a 'hailstorm' in his first Grand Prix Race in a Ferrari Dino *(above)*. A stone damages his radiator and retires him. Dan teams up with Tony Brooks to race a Ferrari 250TR 59 in the Tourist Trophy at Goodwood in 1959 *(below)*. After various vicissitudes they finish fifth.

The British Grand Prix is a disappointment for Gurney both in 1960 at Silverstone with BRM (above) and in 1962 at Aintree with Porsche (below). In both races he is still running at the finish but lapped, placing tenth and ninth respectively.

You see Dan Gurney both coming and going in the wet Belgian Grand Prix at Spa in 1965 (preceding pages). Jesse Alexander catches him on his way to tenth place after a pit stop. In 1968 Dan cadges a one-off drive from Brabham at Zandvoort (above, next to Jo Siffert) but retires with a cranky throttle slide. His forceful drive from pole at Zandvoort in 1964 for Brabham (below) is cut short by steering problems.

Gurney's AAR Eagle V-12 is leading Mike Spence's Lotus BRM at Watkins Glen in 1966 (above). Gurney qualifies well back and retires with clutch trouble. Squaring up with Jim Clark on the front row at Spa in 1967 (below), Gurney is surprised by an early starting flag in a race in which he recovers to take the victory. With power by Chevrolet and an impressive wing, the AAR McLeagle (overleaf) is pictured by Bob Tronolone on its way to fourth in the Can-Am race at Riverside in October 1969.

As the pack comes up through Echo Valley at Bridgehampton in September 1968 the Weslake-Ford-powered McLeagle is among the leaders (opposite). Dan finishes sixth in this, the first Can-Am race of the season. At Sebring in the 1966 12-Hour Race (above) Gurney is disqualified after pushing his Ford Mark II when in sight of a second-place finish. In 1970 Dan, seen neck and neck with team-mate Denny Hulme in M8D McLarens (below), wins two of three races he drives for the McLaren team. In this one at Watkins Glen, however, problems demote him to ninth.

Clockwise from top left, Dan Gurney hobnobs with Roger Penske (left) and Carroll Shelby in the pits at Riverside, takes the wheel of the Arciero Lotus 19 at Riverside in 1962, relishes his success for Brabham at Rouen in 1964 and poses for Max Le Grand.

Clockwise from top left, Dan checks the engine of his Formula 1 Brabham, sits in the Cobra coupé at Le Mans while its plugs are changed, checks the tyre temperature of his Eagle at Indy in 1969 and compares notes with Jim Clark at Indianapolis in 1967.

In an unfamiliar silver helmet Dan Gurney tries out the back-up car he drives in the 1963 Indianapolis 500-mile race (above) after damaging his primary Lotus on qualification day. In 1964 the Lotuses at Indy have Ford twin-cam power (below) but Dan's car is withdrawn after team-mate Clark experiences trouble with his Dunlop tyres.

Feeling overshadowed by the attention given to Clark in the Lotus team, Dan runs a Lotus-Ford with his own team at Indy in 1965 (above). A hidden engine fault stops his challenge that year. In December 1969 Dan jousts at Riverside with the Lola-Chevy of Mark Donohue (below), finishing third. Donohue represents a challenge from a new generation of drivers.

CHAPTER 5

They call it endurance

'Ferrari was throwing me in at the deep end,' Dan said. They don't get much deeper than the Targa Florio. One of the most challenging races ever devised, it was run on roads twisting up into the Madonie hills on the north coast of the rocky island of Sicily from the small town of Cefalu, east of Palermo. In 1959 the Targa would be run over 14 laps of a network of 44.7 miles of these narrow, bumpy roads – the *Piccolo Madonie* circuit.

Among the 1959 Targa starters facing a total distance of 626 miles, just over 1,000 kilometres, was Dan Gurney in only his second race for the official Ferrari team. Dan respected not only the race but also its wonderful history: 'The Targa was just glorious. I'd never been to a track like that, with a history that went back to 1906 – all the great names and all their achievements from Mercedes and Bugatti to Alfa Romeo and Ferrari – what a fabulous place!'

Dan had to get to grips with this incredible circuit: 'Talk about a job of learning! Trying to absorb so much taxed your ability to concentrate. It's very difficult and challenging because so many of its hundreds of turns seem virtually the same as the ones before. You couldn't tell if you were approaching a straightaway or a hairpin. The turn looked the same, the surroundings looked the same and the drop-offs on the outside of the road looked the same.

'I started out as a passenger in a *muletta*,' Dan continued, 'an older Ferrari sports car, a 2-litre Mondial four-cylinder. Phil Hill drove me around and, well, scared the dickens out of me. The routine was that once that was over with – if I had survived that – I became the driver with Cliff Allison as my passenger. I would be surprised if he wasn't a basket case by the time we'd finished.' Emboldened by the experience, Allison then went on a solo lap, at the end of which he demolished the Mondial against a bridge abutment. This so discomfited him that he elected not to drive in the race. Practice continued with rented Fiats.

The preceding pages depict Dan's drives in the very quick Birdcage Maserati in 1960 at the Nürburgring (in colour), where he wins with Stirling Moss, and at Buenos Aires, where he retires after scaring the Ferraris. Here he prepares to be flagged off at the start of the 1964 Targa Florio in a Ford-powered Shelby Cobra. A sister Cobra is next in line.

In the tradition of the point-to-point races of the turn of the century the 50-strong Targa field was started at half-minute intervals. Dan Gurney was at the wheel of the last car to leave the line. It was a new-type Testarossa with a more powerful engine. 'For some reason Enzo Ferrari had given me a good car,' Dan mused. 'I think Enzo liked to see young guys that could make the old timers really squeeze themselves!'

Dan's best practice lap had been misleadingly slow because he'd stopped to comfort and reassure Giorgio Scarlatti, marooned on the circuit after a hair-raising moment when a wheel flew off into the underbrush. Thus it was all the more sensational when Dan set the fastest time for the first race lap at 45:01, a margin of eight seconds quicker than Behra. On the second and third laps he held the lead, but an ominous sign was Gendebien's early retirement with failed rear-axle gears. This too retired Dan Gurney – but they knew he'd been there. 'I had established myself as being someone to reckon with in the team, which was wonderful.'

Porsche won in 1959, setting the scene for a sharp rivalry in the Targa between the two teams that had prancing horses on their emblems. Porsche won in 1960 too, and in 1961 it teamed its newly signed Dan Gurney with Jo Bonnier in a handsome roadster, so new it was unpainted. They brought it home second behind a new mid-engined Ferrari. Re-powered with an enlarged version of its Grand Prix eight, the roadster came back for another try in 1962.

Also new for '62 was a Porsche-designed disc brake which was – to put it charitably – erratic in operation. As Gurney put it dryly, 'It was an unsuccessful idea.' On his second lap he came over the brow of a hill and saw, down below, a right-hand turn and a low bridge flanked by stone walls: 'I put on the brakes, then let off the brake, but they didn't let up, which happened fairly frequently with this Porsche. I arrived there backwards, then – *bam*! This wall flopped over, crashed down. The car stayed on the road.' Dan limped to the next service depot along the route and had a rear wheel replaced, but the suspension was too badly damaged for the car to continue.

Dan's next trip to Sicily for the Targa was his last, in 1964. By now the experienced European campaigner, he was both driver and unofficial 'tour director' for the team of Shelby Cobras that arrived on the island in search of valuable GT category points in their season-long campaign against Ferrari. Thus a week before the race he was all the more mortified to arrive not at Palermo, near the circuit, but at Siracusa, on the south-east coast as far away as possible. 'So we drove across the island,' Dan recalled.

They used both their rented Fiat 2300 and Ford Cortinas to recce the circuit, Jerry Grant for the first time. So demanding was this exercise that they made a discovery; Dan said: 'We found out that if someone spoke up while you were driving, it derailed your thought process. You lost your concentration. You didn't know what section of the track you were on. So we had to say, "Look, no speaking. Just watch." That was the sort of concentration you needed to be able to learn that track.'

That Grant was a fast learner was demonstrated by their performance in the Targa, raced over 10 laps in 1964. By the sixth lap they were second overall in the open Cobra roadster, hardly the most suitable car for the Madonie mountains. Suspension failure dropped them back but Gurney/Grant still eked out an eighth-place finish and valuable GT points.

Gurney contributed to a maximum points scoring in his first official outing for the Ferrari factory team at Florida's Sebring in 1959. There he was teamed with Chuck Daigh for the 12-hour race on airport runways and adjacent access roads. 'During practice a rain shower hit Sebring,' Dan recalled. 'I was on the back airport straightaway, probably 150 yards behind Phil Hill in one of the other Ferraris, and we're going down there good and fast. He ran into one of the big puddles out there and started veering off to one side. The spray was 25 feet high. He was going sideways, out of control, and spun right off the straight. Having seen that I'd slowed down enough but I nearly went the same place he did. That feeling of losing control on a straightaway sort of stands your hair on end, even though you've got a helmet on. It's a very unpleasant feeling.'

Unpleasant as well was Dan's feeling after taking the first stint at the wheel of the Testarossa. He'd not paid enough attention to his seating position and was suffering even worse discomfort than he had during his rainy test at Monza: 'I could barely get out of the car. It was as though I had been doing deep-knee bends, not all the way down and not all the way up, for an hour and 20 minutes. And you really had to stomp on the brakes in those days. The wall in front of the pits was probably no more than 2½ feet high. I could barely get over that!

'And my foot was on fire. I had worn a hole right through my crepe-soled shoe. My foot wasn't bleeding but it was getting close. I stuck it in a bucket of cold water right away and thought, "Boy, this is going to be interesting if I have to go the course."' Luckily for the limping Ferrari new boy, Phil Hill and Olivier Gendebien had trouble with their Ferrari and were told to take over his car, which Daigh had been driving in the meantime. 'So my timing was pretty good!' He and Daigh shared victory at Sebring with Hill and Gendebien.

At Sebring in March 1960 Dan again drove Italian machinery but of a decidedly different ilk. He'd been engaged as driver by a new team, Camoradi, set up by Lloyd 'Lucky' Casner with the backing of Goodyear. Camoradi in turn had contracted with Maserati to race a new sports car that startled everyone with its low build and the multiple-small-tube frame that won it the nickname 'Birdcage'. This, the Tipo 61, was called 'hideously ugly' by *Autosport* and 'flying bathtub' by spectators in Buenos Aires, Argentina, where it made its major international debut in January 1960.

Dan should have raced the Tipo 61 at Nassau in the Bahamas in November 1959. Of three such cars there Gurney's clocked the fastest practice time. But he badly injured a foot in a kart race and was out of racing for the rest of that year. At Buenos Aires 'It didn't take us long to discover that Dan was going to be a real threat with that ugly Maser,' wrote Phil Hill, still with Ferrari. 'I managed to set fastest practice time down there with our 3-litre, but Gurney wasn't far behind me.' Dan led the race but sundry bugs retired the fast Maserati.

For Sebring Camoradi achieved the dream driver pairing of S. C. Moss and D. S. Gurney. 'If it doesn't break, it's got to win,' said Dan of the Tipo 61 before the race. How right he was. He and Stirling led easily until the Birdcage's gearbox broke after eight of the 12 hours.

In 1961 and '62 Porsche had the benefit of the services of Gurney at Sebring. It was to little avail in the first year when his RS61's gearbox failed just after the start, but the result was better in 1962. With Bob Holbert, Dan drove a Carrera GTL coupé to seventh overall and first in class. Headroom was in short supply for Dan in the Abarth-bodied GT car.

Gurney was back in big cars again at Sebring in 1963 with the beginning of the Ford-backed Shelby Cobra campaign. This was early days for the Cobra effort; in the words of Carroll Shelby, 'Just about everything that could go wrong or drop off did go wrong or drop off.' The Cobra Dan shared with Phil Hill failed its rear end after various vicissitudes. In 1964, Dan's Cobra was running a strong fourth near the end of the race when co-driver Bob Johnson tangled with an Alfa in front of the pits. Gurney came back in '65 with a Ford-powered Lotus 19B, which didn't survive the third hour.

At Sebring in 1966 Dan and Jerry Grant paired up to join the Shelby team of Mark II Ford GT cars. 'When everyone ran across the track, jumped in and drove away,' wrote Leo Levine, 'there was one car left on the line. It was Gurney, who in the excitement couldn't locate the switch. After a full minute he found it and screamed off, leaving long black trails of rubber on the concrete. Before 1½ hours had gone by Gurney was in front.'

The Gurney/Grant duo clung to the lead in the big Ford ahead of Ken Miles and Lloyd Ruby in another Shelby car. The chequered flag was ready at the start-finish line. Levine: 'On what would have been his last lap, or at worst his next to last, Gurney's engine had ceased to function and the car rolled to a halt only a few hundred yards from the line. It was a rod bolt that let go, after running 11 hours and 57 minutes. He got out, wondering what to do, when a minor official told Dan to try and push it across. While Gurney was pushing, Miles unlapped himself and went on to win the second consecutive event for himself and Ruby.'

The 'minor official' had been anything but helpful. For more than five years competitors in international events had been barred from pushing cars on the circuit. Had Dan simply left the car where it was, he and Grant would have been classified second overall. Instead, they were disqualified. It was, wrote Levine, 'one of the bigger *faux pas* of the season. Gurney was almost speechless in his disappointment and frustration.'

This was Dan's last start in the Sebring 12-hour. He'd had other long-distance business in Florida as well at the road circuit built inside the banked track at Daytona – for the first time in a February 1962 three-hour race called the 'Continental'. In his Arciero-entered Lotus 19-Climax Gurney took a clear lead and held it to the end – almost. In a finish that became a legend of the sport, the Lotus ground to a halt just short of the finish. 'There was a connecting rod through the side of the block,' said Dan. The legend had it that he then used the starter to motor over the line to win. But he didn't, Dan explained later: 'I didn't use the starter. I just turned left and gravity did the job' on the shallow banking in front of the grandstands.

The 1963 Daytona Continental was the first international race for Shelby's new Cobra team. 'Dan Gurney's car ran into trouble when a Welch plug blew out of the engine shortly before the start,' wrote Carroll Shelby, 'and the water pressure disappeared. Dan's mechanics did a wonderful job of replacing the ruined engine in 90 minutes and got him off only half a lap after the race had started. He made up the handicap and pulled ahead and seemed to demonstrate that the Shelby-Ford Cobra was the fastest machine around, production or otherwise. Then on the 48th lap he was sidelined for good with ignition trouble.'

For 1964 the Daytona race was stretched to 2,000 kilometres. Gurney co-drove a Cobra roadster to fourth overall and second in class, the race's best result for Shelby. In 1965 Dan entered his much-modified Lotus-Ford, sponsored by Pacesetter Homes. With Jerry Grant he led for 809 miles only to retire with engine trouble. In 1966 Dan joined the Shelby-entered Ford GT Mark II effort in a race that was lengthened to a full 24 hours for the first time.

A new driver on the Ford team's strength for 1966, the observant Mark Donohue, couldn't help being impressed by Gurney's performance at Daytona: 'He never used up as many brake pads or rotors as anyone

else, and nobody could understand how he did it, unless he was stopping the car out on the track and replacing the parts himself. He was really spectacular from an engineering standpoint.'

Donohue noticed that Gurney didn't fuss unduly with the chassis set-up of his Mark II Ford: 'Apparently Dan was never too concerned with balancing the car to the nth degree in a long-distance race. He never complained – he just got in the car and drove it. The idea was simply to be comfortable, and he could be because nothing was ever particularly wrong with the set-up. Due to [Ken] Miles's chassis development, the cars were always well balanced. But Dan was always clearly superior – and there were a lot of good drivers to compare him to.'

In '66 Dan came home second behind another Ford after being delayed by a check for damage following the bumping of another car by team-mate Jerry Grant. The Mark II Fords were used again at Daytona in 1967, where Dan teamed with A. J. Foyt for the first time. At Daytona there was no sandbagging in practice; Dan used sticky tyres and extra revs to take pole position against heavy Ferrari and Chaparral opposition. All the Fords retired in the race, however, with faulty gearbox output shafts.

In his final season as a driver, 1970, Dan had one more go at the day-long Daytona race. He co-drove a Ferrari 512S entered by Luigi Chinetti's NART team. Gearbox failure halted their effort soon after the half-way mark. Dan would never compete again in a 24-hour race.

The first-ever Gurney entry in a 24-hour race had also been engineered by NART – at Le Mans in 1958. 'Luigi's team inherited the previous year's Le Mans cars,' Dan said. 'So the car that I ended up driving was one of the 1957 team cars. I ended up equalling Hawthorn's time in the Ferrari from the year before, which meant a great deal to me and probably didn't harm things at all reputation-wise.'

Fascinated by this new environment, seeing all the cars, teams and drivers he'd only read about before, Gurney paid attention to every detail: 'When they fired the Ferraris up I was surprised that they were smoking. There'd be all this blue smoke like the rings were gone. Phil would say, "Don't worry about that. In no time at all that will go away." Sure enough. Pretty soon the pipes were chalk-white. And they said that they made more horsepower after a race than they did before. It was just interesting to see all that.' In the race they were running fourth when Dan's co-driver got caught up in someone's else's accident, fortunately without injury.

Driving in 1959 for the Ferrari works team, paired with Jean Behra, Dan was in the lead at dusk. At that point, wrote Jesse Alexander, 'Gurney felt the gear shift lever come off in his hand. As he went by the signal pits he waved the lever to the observer indicating that he was calling at the pits to get it fixed. He drove into the pits but found no one ready for him and was forced to do one more lap. Next time around – always in second gear and losing precious seconds, he came in again and this time one of the mechanics improvised a lever out of a piece of pipe. Dan said this worked fine, but then headlight troubles dropped him back still further. Finally the car blew its engine after Behra took over.'

The next year saw Dan with Walt Hansgen in a Cunningham-entered Jaguar prototype at Le Mans. The untested car was neither quick nor a finisher. The same applied to the Porsche he co-drove in 1961. In 1962 he drove a 250TR Ferrari for Scuderia Venezia. Following an oil-spewing car soon after the start, his windscreen was suddenly opaque. 'We'd made the seat nice and low for the streamlining and I couldn't look over the screen,' Dan said. 'This was one of the only times I'd ever taken off without a rag in my pocket. Finally I ripped the pants leg off my new driving suit and wiped a porthole in the windscreen. I got oil all over my hands, the steering wheel and everything, but I could see so I could start going again.' It was to no avail because the Ferrari soon retired.

Dan was back with NART in a 330LMB Ferrari for 1963, but this too retired. The 1964 race was more rewarding. Paired with Bob Bondurant, Dan drove to fourth overall and first in GT in a Shelby Cobra Daytona coupé, 'despite the fact that the engine ran 12 hours without an oil cooler and the oil temperature was often at 300°F,' said a delighted Carroll Shelby. This was the first race for Cobra CSX2299, which through an error by its Italian coachbuilders had two inches more headroom than its sisters. This also made it the only Daytona coupé that Dan could sit in comfortably. It

returned to Le Mans in 1965 for Dan to drive with Jerry Grant but retired with clutch failure.

In the Ford GT years at Le Mans, Dan (with Grant) retired in the Mark II in 1966 and then (with Foyt) won in 1967. 'The first time I ran there was in 1958,' Dan reflected, 'and I made probably eight attempts [ten, actually]. It's a good race to win, but after I won there I didn't want to run it again.' Nor did he.

In that final victorious Le Mans race Dan deployed lessons he'd learned in the nine previous attempts. Although lapped, Mike Parkes in a Ferrari was pushing behind Gurney, trying to provoke him into running faster. 'Finally,' Dan recalled, 'I said to myself, "Well, OK, Mike, if that's the way you want it." In coming off the Arnage corner I pulled over to the side of the road and stopped on the grass. He pulled off to the side, too, right behind me. There we were, leading a race that wasn't even half over yet. I waited there in the dark for about 20, maybe 30, seconds and he finally decided that this is kind of silly and he took off then and I followed at my pre-established pace. I caught him about ten laps later as our car was simply faster. Ferrari knew then that I wouldn't be pushed into possibly breaking that Ford – although I might have bitten a few years earlier.'

Other endurance races were on the Gurney agenda. One was the Tourist Trophy at Goodwood, where Dan was paired with Tony Brooks in 1959: 'We had nothing but grief. First the brake pedal fell off, then the brakes went out, then a front wheel began locking. Tyre wear was tremendous – and I blew the left rear just one lap from the finish, driving across the line on a flat to take fifth.' Another competitor that day, Carroll Shelby, noted that Dan 'drove with the dash and skill and determination of an old pro.' In 1964 Dan won valuable points for Shelby by finishing third overall and first GT with his Cobra coupé in the Tourist Trophy.

Next to the Targa, one of the most demanding endurance races that Dan faced was the 1,000 kilometres of the 14.2-mile Nürburgring in Germany, the 'granddaddy' of all the world's permanent road circuits. This hugely daunting track had been carved out of the Eifel Mountains in the mid-1920s to help bring tourists to an out-of-the-way part of Germany.

The 1959 1,000-kilometre race at the 'Ring was, Dan

recalled, 'the famous event in which Stirling Moss gave everyone a driving lesson with his Aston Martin. He drove with fellow Briton Jack Fairman. Moss was an ace at the Le Mans start, where all the cars were lined up on one side of the track and we had to run across, jump in and start the engine. He'd just smoke everybody, time and time again. I really tried hard – but at the 'Ring he was gone! It was amazing. Moss was just very, very special, at the peak of his form in those days.

'In the Ferrari team Phil drove with Olivier Gendebien, and Jean Behra was teamed with Tony Brooks. I drove with Cliff Allison. In the race I fought for second and took some pride in actually reeling Stirling in a little bit. Then, of all things, the clutch started to slip.' Dan learned a lesson from Allison, who during his next stint saved the clutch by shifting without it. Between them they managed a fifth-place finish.

In 1960 the amazing Moss was on Dan's side; both were driving a Birdcage Maserati for Camoradi at the 'Ring. Dan was wearing the white-striped blue helmet that would prove so unlucky at Zandvoort two weeks later. Stirling took the lead on his first stint but Dan, in the next, had to pit with an oil line problem.

Wrote Moss, 'Our comfortable lead melted into a half-lap deficit before Dan belted off again to begin a wonderful drive in the rain and fog. On the 24th lap he was 1 minute 35 seconds behind. He cut it to 47 seconds on lap 25, then to 15 seconds, and on the 28th lap he went past the pits, to enormous and well-earned applause, in the lead again from the Porsche and the Ferrari. Two laps later he handed over to me. I crossed the line to win my third consecutive 1,000-kilometre race.

'I could not have done it without Dan Gurney's wonderful driving,' Moss added generously. He put it in writing, too. A Moss photo on Dan's office wall bears the dedication, 'To my best-ever co-driver. You were great!' He shared this view with others, including Denis Jenkinson, who wrote that Moss 'paid Dan Gurney the finest compliment he could when he said afterwards that he really enjoyed the race because it was so nice to have a co-driver who could keep up the pressure. Previously one has been justified in saying, "Moss wins the 1,000 kilometres of Nürburgring", but this year one can truly say, "Moss and Gurney win the 1,000 kilometres".'

'Not too shabby,' Dan smiled in recalling. 'When we could do that, drive together, we felt like we could whip the world! Line 'em up – we would just knock 'em down one after the other. There was no doubt. It was just a fabulous feeling. I was very fortunate: I shared a car with Behra, I shared a car with Brooks and I shared cars with Stirling Moss on several occasions – a pretty strong list, that, and it was a fabulous experience.'

For Gurney the motor racing enthusiast the 'Ring race had an extra dimension as well. The team manager was Italy's famous 'Silver Fox', a great motorcycle racer in his day, Piero Taruffi. And their Maserati was tended by Guerrino Bertocchi, who was Fangio's mechanic when he was driving for Maserati. 'That bit of historical linkage was great,' Dan reflected. But by now Gurney was making history of his own.

After the Le Mans start at midday at Goodwood for the 1959 Tourist Trophy, Ferrari-mounted Dan Gurney checks the traffic to his left before setting out to chase Jack Brabham's Cooper Monaco-Climax.

On the open runways of Sebring, Florida (above), an uncomfortable Dan drives his first race for the Ferrari factory team. Later he will take more care over his driving position. At the Nürburgring (below) Gurney chases the Aston Martin of Stirling Moss and learns a lesson in clutch preservation from Cliff Allison. Dan and co-driver Tony Brooks confer at the pit counter during a pit stop at Goodwood (opposite). One such stop introduces the brake problems that mar their bid for a top position.

In the Nürburgring 1,000 Kilometres of 1961 Dan drives a Porsche type 718. He is seen in the Karussell (right) and preparing to leave the pits (opposite) after a long stop to fix an ignition problem. Huschke van Hanstein leans into the cockpit next to co-driver Jo Bonnier. Gurney looks pleased with a more powerful version of the same car for the Targa Florio in 1962 (below) but its novel and erratic brakes contribute to a race-ending encounter with a bridge parapet.

At Bridgehampton in September 1963 Dan Gurney wins the GT race in a Shelby Cobra, scoring points in an internationally recognised event. Stanley Rosenthall captures the drama of a pit stop in which Dan gets a fresh pair of goggles and his engine a fresh dollop of oil. Gurney accepts the Bridgehampton trophy from racing driver and New York restaurateur René Dreyfus. Coming out of the Mulsanne corner at Le Mans in 1965 (overleaf) in the Shelby Cobra Daytona coupé Dan shades his eyes from the setting sun. Jesse Alexander seizes the moment.

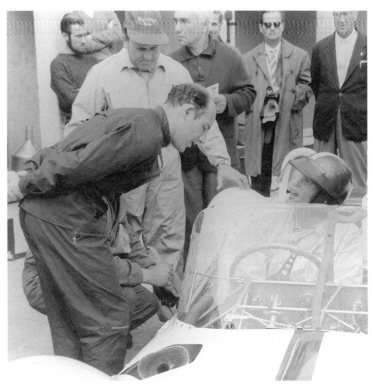

Dan and Phil Hill lend an ear to Tony Brooks at Goodwood in 1959 (opposite, top left). Gurney rates highly the uncanny road-reading abilities of Olivier Gendebien, with whom he talks to Ferrari engineer Carlo Chiti at Goodwood in 1959 (opposite, bottom left). Gurney renders yeoman service as co-driver to Stirling Moss in their winning effort at the Nürburgring with a Camoradi Maserati in 1960 (opposite, top right). In American events, as at Sebring in 1965 (opposite, bottom right), Dan often co-drives with a striped Jerry Grant. At Bridgehampton in 1963 Dan confers with Pedro Rodriguez (above left). At Le Mans (above right) are the 1960 BRM team-mates – (from left) Jo Bonnier, Graham Hill and Gurney, who are also Porsche drivers.

Gurney pedals a Ford GT Mark II very effectively at Daytona in 1966 (above) and places second. Dan takes the lead in the foot race that begins the 1966 Sebring 12 Hours (below). At Sebring he tugs off his helmet during a nocturnal driver change.

CHAPTER 6

Formula 1 the hard way

'**D**an just came up and said, "Let's build a Grand Prix car."' That's the way Carroll Shelby remembered it. Arch-patriot Gurney had always been confident that America could get the job done. When he was asked by Steve McNamara about the prospects for an American GP car as long ago as 1959 he answered, 'They could dominate the scene. There's no reason why they can't. It won't be easy, but they can't do it if they don't try.'

As he spoke those words Lance Reventlow was dedicating a large share of his considerable inheritance to trying. Some had linked Gurney the driver to the Scarab Formula 1 effort, but Dan was unconvinced by its dated front-engined design. He signed with BRM for 1960 instead. The Scarab was a failure but many of its elements displayed the considerable skills of Southern California's engineers and fabricators. With the right design and financing they might be able to get the job done.

Dan Gurney seems to be pleading to the gods for a blessing for his new AAR Eagle Grand Prix effort. Only he and a few close associates are aware of the slenderness of the shoestring on which he launches his bid for Formula 1 success with an American-built car.

Goodyear's backing of AAR had the clear objective of success at Indy. Its first venture into Formula 1 had been with Reventlow, not a rewarding experience. Its tyres were being used in F1 in 1965, but not until the last race of the season would Richie Ginther and Honda deliver Goodyear's first Grand Prix victory. Grand Prix racing would eventually attract Goodyear strongly but it didn't in 1965, when AAR was being set up.

'I don't know whether Goodyear's interested in us doing that or not,' was Carroll Shelby's response to Gurney according to Cynthia Claes. 'Really,' said Carroll, 'the way it came about was just me b-s-ing [Goodyear racing director] Tony Webner into giving us the money. He didn't really want it to happen but I pushed him because Dan really wanted to do it. They went for it as a kind of thank you for us putting that all-American thing together and getting Goodyear known at Indy.'

For Dan the timing was ideal. A new Formula 1 would start in 1966 with engines double the previous size. 'I was probably one of the most vocal against the old 1½-litre limit,' Gurney said. 'I think with bigger engines and higher speeds, Formula 1 regains its prestige.'

Gurney felt strongly that this was the racing category that set the pace for the others: 'Formula 1 is the purest form – and the most varied – in auto racing. It has the fewest restrictions, the most chance for designers to exercise their ability, the most creative brains behind it. And whether you're talking about just driving, or the whole shooting match, it also has the most tradition and prestige. Rightly so, I believe.'

Dan felt he was ready to tackle Grand Prix racing with his own team, he told Joe Scalzo: 'I've put ten years of my life into racing. It hasn't been wasted time by any means. I've kept my eyes open. Sure, we're going to be learning in our first season. But we aren't going over there and look like a bunch of gumps, either. We have a high-talent collection of guys involved. We'll have the equipment, too.'

Plan A had been to build two different cars, one type for Indy and the other for Formula 1, but exigencies of timing and finance precluded this. In fact finance would always be a severe constraint for a programme that depended heavily on a reluctant Goodyear. 'We were a bit naughty even attempting it in the first place,' Dan admitted to Alan Henry. 'We'd got the minimum of backing in every area. I just felt it was an opportunity, as slim as the chances were, that I had to take.'

Hence AAR moved to Plan B: base both cars on the same Len Terry design. 'Our Formula 1 Eagle that we built in '66/'67 was utilising the same form blocks that were in an Indy car of that era,' Dan explained. 'Both the Indy cars and Formula 1 cars carried more fuel then. It was a practical compromise to do that, because we had a very good Indy car and a very good Formula 1 car with the same heritage.' The challenge for the F1 chassis was to reduce its weight; this was progressively achieved.

AAR commissioned and funded the creation of an all-new V-12 engine by England's Weslake, but it well knew that this wouldn't be ready for the start of the 1966 season. As a stand-in it bought four 2.7-litre Coventry Climax fours – engines whose technology, although a decade old, was at least well-known to Gurney, who'd raced ahead of it in his Lotus 19. None produced more than 235bhp.

Dan Gurney and Carroll Shelby shared the April 1966 photocall for the Grand Prix Eagle, the first AAR product to be publicly displayed. In May the Indy programme took priority but by 13 June, after only half a day of testing at Goodwood, the first GP Eagle was ready to race at the dauntingly fast Spa circuit. At a severe power disadvantage, it was the slowest qualifier. This was the race in which a sudden rainstorm sent cars spinning off on the first lap. 'They were filming the movie *Grand Prix*,' Dan recalled, 'and I was so slow when I got to the accident that Phil Hill passed me with the camera car.

'I was very thirsty before that race,' Dan continued, 'so I consumed quite a bit of water.' Soon this – combined with the throbbing vibration of the Climax four – created a stressed situation, he told Tim Considine. 'You'd think you'd be able to wet your pants, right? Could not do it. Absolutely could not do it. No way. So the next thing that happens is you say, "If I don't stop, something's going to burst." I mean, you're talking about a lot of pain. So you stop.'

Gurney rolled to a halt along the Ardennes roadside, picking his spot with care: 'There weren't many spectators along that section. Just some people by a farmhouse.' Leaving his engine idling, he blocked a tyre with a rock and stepped aside to relieve himself. Resuming the Eagle's first Grand Prix, Dan came home seventh, although without enough completed laps to be classified.

Dan's commitment to the Formula 1 effort was such that he spent the summer of 1966 in Europe, working with the team. It was based at Weslake in Rye, where 'AAR' was suitably redubbed 'Anglo American Racing'. Weslake's engine was slow in coming, so AAR at Santa Ana tweaked the Climax to extract 255 horsepower for the late-season races.

At a circuit with a lot of memories for Dan Gurney, France's Reims, the Eagle flew again. The fast road course was lucky for Dan, who scored the Eagle's first finish in the points with fifth at the flag. Goodyear shipped in some improved tyres and chassis improvements were made for the following British GP at Brands Hatch. There the Eagle-Climax was a revelation.

'Despite our weak Climax four-cylinder,' said Dan

after the race, 'we qualified on the front row of a grid that saw Jimmy Clark and Graham Hill in the second row and John Surtees in the third. It meant that the car had arrived. It justified the faith of our sponsors, the hopes of American fans and our own confidence in ourselves. Overnight, we became a force to be reckoned with and the idea dawned very clearly on the competition that when we get our V-12 operating they're going to be in deep trouble. I ran second, third and fourth in the race before retiring with a broken piston.

'Then came the Dutch Grand Prix,' Gurney continued, 'and it only strengthened our conviction. We qualified fourth behind Brabham, Hulme and Clark, but only 0.7 seconds behind Brabham and 0.1 behind Hulme and Clark, and ahead of the Ferrari and BRM two-car teams. It rained the first day of practice and we were fastest in the wet and second fastest the following day when the track was dry. When the race started I fell back to sixth on the opening straightaway simply through lack of power. But we worked our way back up to fourth before a broken oil line forced us out.'

At the Nürburgring Dan drove to a solid fourth before an ignition part failed on the last lap, dropping him to a seventh-place finish. Then at Monza he raced with V-12 power for the first time. Dan: 'The Weslakes weren't happy with the engine performance on the dyno, but they felt we should put the darned thing in the car anyway so that we learned something. It didn't really do particularly well, but we got an attempt under our belt with the 12-cylinder.' Infested with bugs, the engine overheated and Dan called it quits after eight of the 68 laps. It performed no better for Dan at Watkins Glen, so he reverted to the Climax for Mexico City and finished fifth.

The 12-cylinder Eagle had not turned a wheel before arriving at Monza. Dan knew that this was not the way to go motor racing: 'Testing is what knocks out unreliability. We haven't wanted to do the testing in the races themselves, but that's what it keeps boiling down to. Many times what looks to us like an economy move turns out to be more expensive in the long run. It's no insurance against failure. Of course, some of it is plain old luck, too.

'We're trying to do things on a shoestring,' he admitted. 'We're new at this and our engine-building people are new at this. Although collectively we have a lot of experience, this is the first time for us as a team. We've had to be satisfied on a relatively small amount of testing.' Dan raced the Climax-powered car one more time in January in South Africa (retiring with the breakage of a rear suspension mount) before selling it to one of his sponsors, Castrol. AAR didn't want to lose the car – but it needed the money more.

Now it was all up to the V-12. Impressive though this engine was, it was a disappointment to its initiator and sponsor. The 12 was designed and built under the direction of Weslake's stepson, Michael Daniel. The draftsman was Aubrey Woods, whom Dan had met in his BRM days. For the 12 Woods adapted the bottom end of the successful BRM V-8s with which he was intimately familiar. But the crucial power-producing part of the engine was the top end, which – Dan clearly understood and had specified – was to be taken directly from the design of an immensely promising Shell research engine that had been built by Weslake. It indicated that the 12 should deliver at least 450 horsepower.

Somehow, in the rush of designing and building, this requirement was overlooked. When he found this out Dan experienced 'a real sinking feeling. If you're off doing other things, racing, on the other side of the world, and there was no doubt as to the understanding of what was going to be included, and you're away for a month or two and you come back and those decisions had been made – I don't know why it happened. But it did. And I never raced it with 400 horsepower or more.'

Harry Weslake himself was dismayed to find that the engine initially gave no more then 350 horsepower on a jury-rigged dynamometer that was later found to be optimistic. Modifications to the ports produced improvement and the V-12 approached raceworthiness, but was never the dominant force that Gurney had expected – and paid £72,000 for. Nor were enough healthy engines available for use. Thus Dan damped expectations for the 1967 season. 'We are a small outfit,' he said, 'with meagre backing, and spread pretty thin at this point. Any kind of setback will be felt keenly. For instance, if we lose an engine one car probably won't race.'

Against this gloomy forecast the success achieved by AAR in the March 1967 Race of Champions at Brands Hatch was all the more impressive and heartening. The event was run as two ten-lap heats with a 40-lap final. Among the major teams only Lotus and BRM were absent; Cooper, Brabham, McLaren and Honda were all represented. Two Eagle V-12s were entered, one for Dan and one for Richie Ginther.

Said *Autoweek*'s reporter, 'Dan Gurney began early taking everything there was to be had at the Race of Champions.' First on offer were 100 bottles of Lanson champagne for the fastest practice lap. Dan won these with a time that lowered the Brands lap record by 3 seconds and grinned as Harry Weslake enjoyed a sip. Dan then won both heats with Richie third in the first, and second in the second. This assured both of front-row starting positions in the final, which Dan led from flag to flag, holding off a banzai last-lap challenge from Lorenzo Bandini's Ferrari. Richie held second place before retiring with wild vibration from a thrown wheel weight.

'We certainly don't want to start crowing about blowing off the competition at this point,' Gurney warned after Brands. 'We are far from being home free.' But, he added, the victory 'was, frankly, a tremendous thrill. It proves we have not one but two drivers and not one but two cars. It was very exciting to see that Richie and I were able to out-accelerate anything on the starting grid.' Dan's success was hugely popular with the 40,000 spectators, as *Motoring News* reported: 'The crowd showed their appreciation of Gurney's win in no uncertain manner.'

This storming success at Brands Hatch was the prelude to the 60 days in May and June that saw Dan Gurney win at Le Mans and then at Spa. Wrote Denis Jenkinson after the Belgian victory, 'While this was a fine achievement in itself it was doubly praiseworthy for it was at the Belgian GP exactly 12 months before that the first Grand Prix Eagle ran. A lot of teams with years of experience and almost unlimited resources have never equalled this feat.' AAR co-founder Carroll Shelby echoed that assessment: 'I think it was really a

milestone to build that car and go win a race against those odds.'

For the next Grand Prix, the French on the Bugatti Circuit at Le Mans, Bruce McLaren joined Dan on the AAR strength. They qualified well but both had retired by half-distance, Dan when he was battling with Jack Brabham for the lead. The story was similar at Silverstone's British GP, except that AAR's competitiveness seemed to have waned – or the others were getting more into their seasonal stride.

No race of 1967 was more disappointing for Dan than the German GP on the Nürburgring. 'One of the real heartbreakers,' he said. Jim Clark led from pole but was soon in trouble with a deflating tyre. Dan: 'Denny and I both went by. After Adenau bridge you went up a little right and then down to a right-hand turn where, I think, Carel Godin de Beaufort was killed. Then it started to climb up. You were going fast. Up in one of those sections he hit a puddle of water and had a monumental tank-slapper. Boy, he lifted big time and that was it.' Gurney was past and into a dominant lead.

'But then the universal joint broke, on the half shaft. We had a 43-second lead and only three laps to go. I was able to set a new lap record for the race before going out, so we weren't running badly. The 'Ring is fairly rough on equipment, with cars getting airborne quite a bit, and this was probably the source of our problem. Later my mechanic Tim Wall came to me and blamed himself for it, and I said, "Oh, you're crazy." He said, "I should have relieved it because the joint's angularity got to the point where it was touching – on the joint itself."

'I always wanted to win that race at the 'Ring and couldn't do it,' Dan reflected. 'I came reasonably close in '67 with the Eagle. Holding the unofficial Formula 1 lap record there in '62 – they didn't break that year or in '63. And in '67 they didn't break it, in '68 they didn't break it. So I had it for four years altogether. Better than nothing. That place was really the epitome of the sport in a way. I liked it. I liked to come to grips with it. It's too bad that it didn't work out.'

Bruce McLaren's own BRM-powered car was ready for the next race in Canada so AAR had only a singleton entry there for Dan. Retirements helped him to a third-place finish behind Brabham and Hulme in a damp race at Mosport. Two Eagles were ready for Monza in September, where Ferrari's sole entry freed popular aristocrat Lodovico Scarfiotti to team up with Dan. Neither's engine lasted more than five of the 68 laps. Dan led – but only for the first two circuits.

A shortage of engines meant that the final North American races were contested by only one Eagle-Weslake. This was a disappointment for Dan, especially because he had hoped to have an extra car ready early enough for his Le Mans partner A. J. Foyt to see whether he fancied this kind of racing. At both Watkins Glen and Mexico Dan and his Eagle were fast, qualifying third fastest, but retired. At the Glen a suspension breakage was at fault. At Mexico City a tricky wave of the starting flag caused Jim Clark to hesitate and Dan ran the nose of his car right into Clark's exhaust pipes, finishing the Eagle's radiator – a sad end to a chiaroscuro season.

Stretching his meagre resources to the limit, Gurney decided to set up an engine-building and car-preparation unit of his own at Ashford, 15 miles north-east of Rye. Aubrey Woods joined him there to try to get to grips with the V-12 engine, which had been manufactured neither accurately nor consistently enough. In the meantime Dan made a low-key appearance on New Year's Day at Kyalami for the 1968 season opener. He was only eighth when he retired at three-quarters distance.

AAR entered Dan for the Brands Race of Champions but the team was a no-show. The Spanish GP was skipped in favour of the following event at Monaco, where the Eagle was depressingly slow. Dan only squeaked on to the last row of the abbreviated Monegasque grid by virtue of AAR's acceptance, at last, as an official works team. Shortages of sparks and oil pressure retired him early.

The Belgian, Dutch and French races were missed to give the Ashford operation time to get into gear. Their first engine was ready for the British GP in July at Brands Hatch. AAR's lack of development showed. Other teams had moved forward, especially in using the new-fangled wings. Dan could only qualify equal sixth with Stewart's Matra-Ford. He fell right to the back at

the start, completing only one-tenth distance. The race engine had oiled the clutch and it wouldn't hold.

Wet weather at the Nürburgring made practice a lottery and Gurney was back in tenth place. By the end of the first lap he had halved that and during the third lap he was up to third place in dire weather conditions: 'It was raining like nobody's business. I cut a tyre and had to drive a little over seven miles with a flat. And then we had six nuts holding the wheel on, so I was *way* back. My pit told me that I ran almost every lap after that faster than the leader, for the whole race. I would say that that might have been one of my better drives. Finished ninth – a terrific race.' Dan would never drive in anger at the 'Ring again.

Although at Monza Dan was only 1.5 seconds slower that the Honda of pole-sitter Surtees, that placed him 12th on the grid in a closely competitive field. In the race he battled up to ninth but, in an experience that was frustratingly and embarrassingly similar to the V-12's debut two years earlier, the engine expired with temperature up and oil pressure down. Worst of all, for a driver and team owner who lived by speed and the stopwatch, he had not been competitive.

Monza was the final fling for AAR's Grand Prix effort. A completely new car had been abuilding at Santa Ana in readiness for 1969. But when doing his sums in November Dan realised that he didn't have enough funding to support another Formula 1 season. There was a reason for that, he told Tim Considine: 'The director of Goodyear Racing took a fair amount of advice from my former partner, Carroll Shelby. I think, in their infinite wisdom, they decided that they'd dry up the stream. They wanted me to come back and try and help them more in their Indy efforts. And the best way to get me back was to cut off Formula 1 funding, right?'

Dan announced that AAR would no longer contest Formula 1. 'Didn't have enough money. Didn't have enough engine. Didn't have enough anything,' he said later to Considine. 'There comes a point where the old college try and the never-give-up stuff becomes really hard to justify and reality starts raising its head. I had to make a decision whether to continue over there or continue over here. I couldn't do both any longer. Never could do both efficiently. Plus, I had a marital problem that just added fuel to that little fire. So that's where it just got to be too much.

'We knew we were stretching it and asking for a great deal,' Gurney continued, 'but it was an opportunity we had and we all wanted to do it – and we bloody well did it. We won two Formula 1 races and achieved much more success than most of the pundits thought was possible. We whipped the Ferrari factory and everybody else at Brands Hatch. And then at Spa we whipped them all. I look back on the whole Eagle experience as being more miraculous than it was disappointing. I thought it was very, very good.'

During Monza practice Dan had tried the spare F1 car of another Goodyear-linked team, McLaren. On the Monday after the race he agreed a deal to race that car backed by his major sponsor, Olsonite, in the North American GPs. At Canada's demanding St Jovite circuit Gurney brilliantly demonstrated that his skills were intact by outqualifying Hulme and McLaren in similar cars and tying for third fastest with Jo Siffert's Walker Lotus. However, overheating retired him early.

At both Watkins Glen and Mexico City Dan split the qualifying times of his team-mates, Hulme being the faster on both occasions. Dan held third at the Glen until a slow puncture dropped him to fourth at the finish, Surtees elbowing past. In the Mexican race he'd risen to third as well when a rear wishbone failed.

In 1970, with an empty seat left by Bruce McLaren's death, McLaren engaged Gurney for three more Grand Prix races. This produced anything but ideal conditions for Dan to get to know the new M14A-Ford. His qualifying positions were dismal by his standards at Zandvoort, Clermont-Ferrand and Brands Hatch. In the first and last races he retired but at Clermont, on a true road course many have likened to a mini-Nürburgring, Dan was outstanding. From 17th on the grid he rose to sixth at the finish.

Thus ended Dan Gurney's Formula 1 career after a total of 86 races. He had four wins, three pole positions and six fastest laps to his credit. He had finished second eight times and third seven times. His best World Championship years were 1961, when he was tied for third with Moss, and 1965 when he was fourth. Dan was fifth in the world rankings in 1962 and '63 and sixth in 1964. His total points haul was about the same as those of Mike Hawthorn and Alberto Ascari – the kind of company Dan would appreciate.

'Dan Gurney is in the front rank of the few Americans who have contributed richly to the World Championship scene,' wrote Louis Stanley after Dan's withdrawal from GP competition. 'His approach to racing is that of a master craftsman. He will be greatly missed. He must be granted his place in any roll-call of racing giants. He must be judged, as anyone should be, on the merits of his finest races. In size and ability he stands head-and-shoulders above the majority of rivals on the grid. Like Stirling Moss, it seems illogical that such talent should not be rewarded with the supreme title.'

Throughout his career Dan never quite had the equipment to make a real run at that title. Said his erstwhile mechanic Jo Ramirez, 'Jimmy Clark used to say that if Dan had the right car, no one would see him.' Speaking to Barrie Gill, Gurney was philosophical: 'Ferrari had their best year after I left and BRM their best year once I'd gone. And the same thing happened with Jack. But that's hindsight. I've often laughed about the way other outfits were successful after I had left. But hell, that's the way it goes.'

Debut race for the Grand Prix Eagle is at rainy Spa in 1966. At the end of that season Gurney presents and races his Formula 1 Eagle with its Weslake-built V-12 engine for the first time at Monza (overleaf left). Michael Daniel with striped shirt and spectacles is on the left and cowboy-hatted team manager Bill Dunne on the right. Harry Weslake joins Dan for a glass of champagne after the American won 100 bottles for setting the fastest lap in practice for the Race of Champions at Brands Hatch in 1967 (overleaf right). Fortunately Dan hadn't yet developed his champagne-spraying technique.

At Canada's Mosport Park in September 1967 Gurney finishes third with his AAR Eagle in a damp race. In the marquee that serves as a garage he confers with mechanics Tim Wall, left, and Jo Ramirez. A race fan outside the marquee has the right idea.

Bill Dunne looks into the camera before the first race start at Spa in 1966 of a Grand Prix Eagle (below left). A year later at the same daunting road circuit Gurney brakes heavily (below right) on his way to victory in the Eagle's only championship Grand Prix success. At Monza in 1967 (above) the Eagle-Weslake completes only four laps before suffering engine failure.

The new 3-litre Grand Prix formula is well into its stride by the time of the German Grand Prix in August 1967. Among the starters snapped by Bernard Cahier (preceding spread) are Denny Hulme in a Repco-Brabham (2), Bruce McLaren in an Eagle Weslake (10), John Surtees in the white Honda, Jackie Stewart in a BRM (11) and Dan Gurney (9), accelerating from his fourth-place starting position. Dan easily leads the demanding race but is retired by a broken universal joint. At Monaco in 1967 (right) the Eagle flies in the early laps but is soon let down by a failure of the drive to the fuel injection metering unit. Dan attracts some sidewalk supervision as he checks for a solution to the problem. Gurney's bird comes good for Spa in 1967 (above) where he shrugs off fuel-system worries to defeat all comers in an historic all-American victory.

With his own Eagle running short of reliability and resources Dan has three Grand Prix drives with the McLaren team at the end of 1968. His best finish is fourth at Watkins Glen (opposite, top) where he is being lapped by team leader Bruce McLaren (opposite, bottom).

At St Jovite in Canada Dan drives a McLaren M7A-Ford in September 1968 (below). He is leading team-mate Denny Hulme but a radiator problem ends his race. Dan appreciates the McLaren rides but is frustrated (right) by the team's reluctance to accommodate his ideas on car preparation.

CHAPTER 7

Trans-Am to Can-Am

Dan Gurney was rightly famed for his versatility. His successes in USAC races, Grand Prix racing and endurance contests demonstrated that he was not only quick but also adaptable. 'The guy was a phenomenal race driver to my way of thinking,' said another racer with a similar reputation, Mario Andretti. 'Dan Gurney could drive anything. He could drive stock cars, could drive sports cars, Indy cars, could drive Formula 1.'

Several motivations underlay the breadth of Gurney's commitment to motor racing. Dan the driver had a passion for the sport. He was curious about all aspects of it and eager to experience what it had to offer. He felt that every variety of the sport had something to teach him and, from his first moment behind the wheel, he was eager to learn.

Also, Gurney relished being the first to do something

From third on the grid Dan Gurney storms into the lead at the first Can-Am race of the 1967 season at Bridgehampton. He is chased by the new McLarens of Denny Hulme (5) and Bruce McLaren (4). Behind them are Jim Hall's winged Chaparral and the Lola-Chevys of Mark Donohue and John Surtees. Fuel-injection problems knock Dan out early.

in racing. As he said to Peter Manso, 'I enjoy exploring new grounds, or doing things that people haven't done before, or not many people can do, or setting records, no matter what kind of thing it might be.' As we saw in the preceding chapter he set goals for himself at Indy: to be the first to win in a rear-engined car or the first Grand Prix driver to win the 500-mile race. Though he did not say so, we may also be sure that he wanted to be the first to win it with a stock-block engine. That he failed to achieve these goals is secondary; he enjoyed setting them as a challenge to himself.

Above all, Dan Gurney took part in many aspects of the sport because he wanted to test his skills against those of other drivers. And if they didn't want to compete in his patch, he would compete in theirs! This was a powerful motivating factor throughout his career on the track. As he said to Barrie Gill, 'I aim for a win where you beat the best guys there are without them being in any kind of trouble. But that kind of race doesn't happen very often.'

Dan took a great deal of pleasure from the opportunities he had throughout his 15 years of racing to compare the skills of his many team-mates and rivals over that period. How many drivers are in a position to discuss the relative abilities of, say, Tony Brooks and Junior Johnson? Johnny Rutherford and Jean Behra? Curtis Turner and Ricardo Rodriguez? Gurney could, because he'd raced them. 'This is a very human sport,' he said. 'And that's what I think the fans like to see – the human aspect of it, who is the best driver on a given day.'

His appetite for fine machinery was yet another motivation for Dan's wide choice of racing rides. He was interested in all aspects of automobiles and knowledgeable about most aspects as well as a result of his autodidact attention to detail. His friend and frequent colleague Jerry Eisert called Gurney 'a real good mechanic, which is a big help to me. He's exceptionally sharp about the chassis; he can come in after a few laps and explain just how the chassis should be set up for the race track.'

Not all mechanics or teams were as appreciative as Eisert of Dan's interest in and attention to the mechanical side of his car. Some felt that he was often in danger of fixing something that wasn't broken. But Dan was unrepentant: 'I know that I had a reputation of sorts for messing around with the car too much. It's justified in many ways. But I do think that this "engineer without portfolio" thing has been misinterpreted. You have the choice of either trying to learn or sitting there like a bump on a log and just taking what people give you.'

We recall that the latter option was debarred by his experiences with BRM in 1960. Ever afterward Dan would take a personal interest in elements of the car that had a bearing on his personal safety. 'When you boil it all down,' he said, 'this quest for knowledge is motivated by a safety consideration. If you've a car that is operating properly you can go faster a whole lot safer than you can with a car that you're going to carry on your back, so to speak.'

Engines rated high among the elements of a car that deeply interested Dan. When he set up AAR he took care to provide it with a first-class engine-development facility, something most other Indy car – and indeed most Grand Prix car – builders lacked. He wanted it not only because it could give his cars a performance edge but also because he was profoundly interested in and

sensitive to engines: 'I can usually sense an imminent problem in an engine a little sooner than most of the drivers, I believe, and can shut down before we have the full catastrophe.'

From the first flat-head Ford V-8 that he hot-rodded, engines have always figured prominently in the Gurney career. Other successful racing drivers have set up companies to make cars. Bruce McLaren, John Surtees, Jack Brabham and Jim Hall are some who come to mind. But did any of these make complete racing engines from scratch, as Dan did for his Formula 1 car? Even with the help of outside contractors? To find drivers who did you have to go back to the Maserati brothers and Enzo Ferrari.

Engines were at the heart of another Gurney project, nicknamed 'Alligator' for its low build and menacing aspect. Motorcycle fanatic Gurney had a special R&D unit at Santa Ana developing an ultra-potent single-cylinder motorbike. 'The challenge is to build the best single there has ever been,' said Dan. A lifelong off-road rider and sometime competitor in desert bike races, Dan was his own best judge of whether this goal had been achieved.

Involved as he was with the cars he raced, Gurney felt a special bond with them. 'There is almost a human friendship that you might develop,' he said. 'You're alone out there on a race track with the car and you're going through a battle together. It's you and your machine. You have won a race and the car's on display somewhere and you come back and see it; it brings back the memories of being together through all these conditions which are a bit like a battle.'

Although we can understand Dan Gurney's attraction to different forms of the sport and his reasons for the diversity of his involvement, we can still be awestruck by his ability to cope with the characteristics of so many kinds of cars. He was a quick study, he told Dale Kistemaker: 'You get attuned; a lot of it is timing. The size of a vehicle, the weight, the polar moment of a vehicle become almost second nature to you. The steering, the wheels and the suspension become extensions of your own body functions and nerve endings, so that you can really feel what's going on and you become part of that vehicle. Sort of bolted into it.'

The contrasts could be great in practice, Dan continued: 'If you are tuned into a light, nimble Formula 1 car and then get into a Grand National stock car, for instance, it feels as though when it goes to do something, it almost writes you a letter! It seems things take a long time to happen. But that doesn't make it any easier to drive.'

Apart from his early outing at Meadowdale Dan's first stock-car drive was at Daytona in 1962 in a car prepared by Holman-Moody. 'I was amazed when I first got into the Ford,' Dan recalled. 'There wasn't much difference in the way it handled compared to sports cars. The biggest difference was in the braking. These big cars were harder to stop. Of course it was different from driving a sports car. There's a lot more car in front of you and NASCAR's big roll cage around you. The doors are bolted shut and you have to crawl through the side window. I felt different – not more confident, but maybe safer.'

Learning the tricks of the NASCAR trade on the high-banked tracks of the American Southland was another attraction for the curious Gurney, he told Peter Manso: 'A lot of people have heard of the tremendous speeds and the problems of drafting at Daytona Beach. These stories have a way of being magnified and you really have to find out for yourself. Are all these stories true or aren't they? There are a lot of difficulties in any kind of racing and they are not all the same; some of them are unique to stock car racing.' For example, he added, 'these boys are not afraid to tap you if they think they can get past. It adds a new element. You have to watch out for anyone close to you.'

Ralph Moody of Holman-Moody did his best to help Dan acclimatise to this new form of the sport. 'At Atlanta I was driving for him,' said Gurney, 'and was having trouble getting up to decent speeds. So Ralph, who had already retired, got in the car and went out and ran about 4 miles per hour faster than I had been going. Then he came in and said that everything was all right. I just didn't have the feel for it.'

Feel for it or not, Dan achieved some creditable stock car finishes. His record at Riverside was remarkable (see Chapter 8). In the Daytona 500 he finished fifth in 1963 and 14th in 1964. Thereafter his oval-track

NASCAR participation tapered off. He was honest about the reason why: 'I wasn't terribly enthusiastic about running the stockers at Daytona, mostly because I don't like to get beaten. I didn't know the tricks of that trade; didn't know the people I was running with. In every traffic situation or just plain fighting it out, a lot of it is sizing up the driver/car combination. You've got to know what they're going to do, or at least have a pretty good idea, or you're in trouble.'

While getting to know Britain, her circuits, races and drivers during his BRM year of 1960, Dan had a typically Gurneyesque inspiration. Those Jaguars ruling the standard-saloon-car roost could be given quite a scare by an American 'sedan', he thought. Chevrolet had just brought out a new 409-cubic-inch engine for its Impala, so Dan obtained one and brought it to Britain. In the May 1961 Silverstone meeting it did indeed shock the Jaguars, starting from pole and leading easily until a wheel centre pulled out and retired Gurney.

Dan entered the Impala again for Silverstone in July, but this time his entry was rejected, ostensibly over a fault in the homologation paperwork. This left a sour taste in the Californian's mouth, as he wrote to *Autosport*: 'I must admit to being surprised, disappointed and disillusioned by the action which prevented the car from running. This particular car was passed by the scrutineers and accepted for the saloon car event at Silverstone last May. The entire project of entering and racing the Impala was financed by me personally. I will, in time, get over the fact that I spent a lot of time and money in bringing the Impala to Great Britain, but I will not readily forget the suspicion that there may have been some behind-the-scenes sabotage to prevent the Chevrolet from running at Silverstone.'

A more pleasant memory of saloon-car racing in Britain resulted from Dan's entry at Oulton Park in September 1963 in a Ford Galaxie. On a narrow, hilly track to which the big Ford was completely unsuited Dan qualified fastest and won the race – demolishing the class lap record – against Lotus-Cortinas and a similar car driven by Graham Hill.

Similarly competitive racing on American road courses was generated in the late 1960s when the Sports Car Club of America (SCCA) set up its Trans-Am series for the new generation of 'ponycars' patterned after the wildly popular Ford Mustang. When Ford's Mercury Division got its own ponycar in 1967, the Mercury Cougar, it launched a Trans-Am racing programme for it and engaged a spectacular team of drivers: Dan Gurney and Parnelli Jones.

Overbodied compared to its rivals, in four races the Cougar gave Dan one third-place finish at Kent and the victory at Smithfield, Texas, that helped spark his successful summer of '67. In 1968 and '69 he drove a Mustang in four races for Carroll Shelby, his best result a third at Laguna Seca. In 1970 Gurney's AAR was engaged to race Barracudas for Chrysler's Plymouth Division in a Trans-Am programme that failed to reach its stride before budget cutbacks began. In the only race of four that Dan finished he placed fifth.

Cars like these were a far cry from the pure racing machines that Gurney usually raced for AAR and others. From the driving seat of a Ferrari in 1959 Dan had had a front-row seat for the drama of the transition to the rear-engined racing car. Emboldened by his conviction that the front-engined car was history, Dan urged Frank Arciero to put his name down for the new mid-engined sports-racing car being built by Lotus. Although officially named the Monte Carlo in a gentle gibe at Cooper's Monaco, it was always known as the Lotus 19.

'We ended up getting the second one built,' Dan said. 'I just had enormous faith in that car before it even ran. I convinced Frank he ought to buy it, and it turned out to be a fabulous car. A giant-killer kind of car.' Its 2½-litre Climax engine let Dan down in his first drive with it at Riverside but he was the main race winner at Nassau in December 1960. He won the Nassau Trophy again with the Lotus in 1961 and the 3-hour race at Daytona the following February – the one he won by coasting down the banking over the line.

Gurney in the Arciero Lotus with its bold number 96 was a frequent sight on American tracks through 1962. In '61 Dan had to give best to Stirling Moss in a similar car at Laguna Seca – just the kind of contest with a top driver he enjoyed. Dan demolished the lap record in practice. Wins came for Gurney at Kent and Laguna Seca in '62. Looking back on the Lotus Dan recalled it

as 'a great car', but 'we managed to louse it up. I don't think it ever handled quite as good as when it was new.'

By 1963 a few car builders were experimenting with the installation of American V-8s in light mid-engined sports-racing cars. One such was San Franciscan Joe Huffaker, who was building Genie sports-racing cars to take such engines. A Ford-powered Genie was fielded by the team of Easterner Briggs Cunningham, who engaged Gurney to drive it at Kent and Riverside in the autumn of 1963. Neither outing was a success, but the experience of working with the Cunningham team was useful because Dan was about to take delivery of a V-8-powered car of his own.

Gurney's idea was to marry the light, agile Lotus 19 chassis to a modified Ford V-8 – Ford instead of the ubiquitous Chevrolet V-8 because Dan was involved then with both Shelby's Cobra team and the Ford Indy effort. Dan asked Lotus to design a special 19 to take a Ford V-8 engine, this time for his own account. Len Terry made the changes and created the 19B. Gerard Crombac quoted a Chapman colleague about the transaction: 'I was present at the final meeting in Colin's office at the Cheshunt factory, where not only were the technical details thrashed out but also the financial side of the deal. After about one and a half hours Dan showed Colin his hand to seal the agreement and said: "Well, that is the first car I have ever bought where the clutch was an optional extra!"'

With the Lotus 19B Gurney set up his own racing team, engaging ex-Arciero mechanic Bill Fowler as his first employee. Fowler would later have the same role in the creation of AAR. Making its debut at Nassau in December 1963, the new car broke its suspension. The following October Dan won a short race with it at Riverside – which in fact was his only outright win with this car. That same month he was second with the 19B at Laguna Seca.

By now the age of the V-8-powered mid-engined sports-racing car had dawned. Among the companies building bespoke chassis for this purpose was Bruce McLaren's. In 1965 Dan bought a McLaren for his newly formed AAR. He raced it only once at Riverside as a test bed for the new high-performance cylinder heads he had commissioned from Harry

Weslake for the Ford V-8. It went well until a wheel bearing failed.

Although fully committed to its single-seaters, AAR didn't exclude the idea of making sports cars as well. 'If we decide to interest ourselves in sports car racing in the future,' Carroll Shelby told John Blunsden, as they stood next to the AAR McLaren-Ford, 'it will likely be with a car we design and build ourselves.' In 1966 the motivation was created for just such a project: the SCCA's establishment of the Can-Am Challenge Cup for Group 7 sports-racers. Like the Trans-Am, it was the right series at the right time.

If ever a racing series seemed made to order for Dan Gurney, it was the Can-Am. With unrestricted power it was a feast for an engine man. He knew all its Canadian and American race tracks well. Its rich purses attracted the world's best drivers, at various times including Bruce McLaren, Mario Andretti, Denny Hulme, John Surtees, Chris Amon, Phil Hill and Jo Siffert. Here were men worth defeating. It also lured strong teams from Europe, which motivated the patriotic Gurney to mount a defence of his homeland. Yet for Dan and AAR the Can-Am was not a great success.

In the Can-Am the AAR effort was always a day late and a dollar short. Inevitably it took third place behind its Indy and Formula 1 programmes. Although Gurney was by far Ford's strongest flagbearer in the series, the Blue Oval was erratic in its support, to put it charitably. Also enjoying the Can-Am participation of the McLaren and Penske teams, Goodyear had no reason to single out AAR for special support. But Dan entered anyway. How could he not?

Shelby's hopes notwithstanding, AAR was not in a position to design and build a unique sports-racing Eagle – more's the pity. Instead it bought one of Eric Broadley's handsome new Type 70 Lolas. Jerry Grant warmed it up with a win in an SCCA race at Bridgehampton in April 1966, the first victory for a Ford with AAR's special cylinder heads. With the same car at the same track Dan was the winner of the second-ever Can-Am race in September. This would go down in history as the only Ford-powered victory in the Can-Am's nine-year lifetime.

The Bridgehampton win ended a lengthy drought in the Gurney career. Since his Formula 1 victory for Brabham at Mexico City in October 1964 he had won only two other races, both stock car events at Riverside. His international career as a driver had languished during the years of establishing AAR, and Dan knew it: 'I'm not getting a chance to drive enough any more. That's one thing about all this that ends up being a compromise. We're trying to get something else going that means a lot to us all. We are hoping to organise a lot more, but for now we're spread very thin. Not at all as efficient as we'd like.'

In 1966 his mount failed him in every other Can-Am race. He was always fast, with two poles and a fastest lap to his credit, and the AAR turn-out was first class as well, as Frank Litzky reported to readers of *The New York Times*: 'In the cockpit of his royal blue roadster, wearing a gleaming black helmet and white fire-proof racing suit, he looks like a Hollywood version of a Grand Prix driver – handsome, slick, terribly sophisticated. Then he steps out of his car, wearing blue tennis sneakers that are torn, dirty and tired.'

Litzky also revealed Dan's insurance arrangements: 'He carries $150,000-$200,000 in life insurance. And because he is a greater risk than a book-keeper or mechanic or ballet dancer, he pays an extra premium of $15-$20 for each $1,000 of insurance. The cost is steep, but people are surprised that a race driver can buy life insurance at any price. "Insurance companies,' said Gurney, 'have rates for all kinds of nuts."'

A new lighter Lola Mark 3B was acquired for 1967 and a special big-block Ford engine installed but the package was bug-ridden and Dan saw no chequered flags. Nevertheless he and his team worked hard to improve the Lola as fellow competitor Mark Donohue learned. 'When Dan showed up at the next race,' Mark told Paul Van Valkenburg, 'he had a different rear suspension and the car was lots faster. He had moved the control arm brackets around and fabricated new wishbones, probably based on his experiences with the Ford factory team efforts. I didn't understand why, and I was really curious about it.

'Even though I still didn't know him,' Mark continued, 'he seemed like such a likeable guy that I asked him, "Please, would you mind telling me what you've done here?" Dan sat down and said, "Look, we all work really hard in racing to be a little bit better than the next guy. Roger [Penske] has a lot of ins that I don't have, like getting pieces from Chevrolet and cars from Lola. Now maybe I understand suspensions a little better than other people, and that may give *me* some small advantage. I would be stupid to tell that to anyone." I thought that was a really good answer.'

In 1968 Ford failed to deliver promised big-block engines so AAR decided to make a good little car by modifying and lightening a bought-in McLaren M6B so extensively that it received and deserved the name 'McLeagle'. It was not up to the new works McLaren competition, however, and a spotty finisher. A Lola T160 with a big Ford V-8 was quicker under Dan in the last two '68 Can-Ams but no more reliable. This was promising, however, so Gurney banked on a commitment by Ford to supply even better engines for 1969. At the eleventh hour, they failed to materialise.

Dan reverted to the McLeagle for '69, now fitted with two high wings. Experiments with a new three-valve engine failed to flower so Dan deserted the Ford camp and installed a big-block Chevrolet. With this he finally finished a race, placing fourth at Riverside in spite of a leaking head gasket. Here was some hope for 1970, he wrote to his fan club: 'We still intend to try and blow the New Zealanders back across the ocean, which will be a formidable task.' Yet Riverside was fated to be Dan's last Can-Am in an AAR-prepared car.

Gurney joined the New Zealanders instead. At a Michigan race in 1969 he had been loaned the third spare McLaren M8B and piloted it with ease from the back of the grid to a third-place finish. After Bruce McLaren's death in a testing accident Dan was the obvious choice to pair with Denny Hulme in 1970 in the new M8D McLaren.

Dan found that the McLaren 'really did have an extra dimension in roadholding and handling which gave it a real advantage through twisty road sections where the driver could go to work with confidence.' He put this to good use at the opening Canadian races at Mosport and St Jovite, both of which he won from pole, also collecting fastest lap at Mosport. After several pit stops Dan was only ninth in his third race for McLaren at Watkins Glen.

That was his penultimate drive for McLaren (he drove an F1 car for them in Britain the following weekend) for their alliance was unravelling. The talk at the time was of sponsorship conflicts between AAR's Castrol backing and McLaren's Gulf support. Behind this, however, were more profound issues. When Gurney saw chances to alter his car's set-up for the better, he was forbidden to do so by the McLaren management. He found this 'a little difficult, after you've been running your own team.'

Dan wasn't completely comfortable with the McLaren crew because, as he said, 'We had been competitors both in the sponsorship arena and on the race track for so many years.' Nevertheless McLaren was pressing Dan to make a wholehearted commitment to its England-based team for Formula 1, Can-Am and even Indianapolis. Realising that this would be 'a full-time job', Gurney 'was faced with the choice of going with McLaren and losing AAR, really.' And AAR was his future.

One other factor contributed to Gurney's decision to step down from McLaren, as he told Phil Llewellin: 'I won a Can-Am race and didn't get any satisfaction out of winning. Who had I whipped? That was a strong feeling. I started to realise that certain people weren't there any more to compete against, and I was lonely because of that. I always wanted to race with the best – Jimmy and Stirling and drivers with that sort of reputation. If they're not around any more...' Dan Gurney was running out of mountains to climb.

Jo Ramirez stands by as Dan boards the doubly-winged and Chevy-powered McLeagle at Michigan International Speedway in September 1969. Problems with the car lead him to accept a ride instead in the third spare McLaren. He races it from the back of the grid to third at the finish.

At the May 1961 Silverstone meeting Dan Gurney presents his personal Chevrolet Impala for the production saloon car race. It easily leads the previously all-conquering Jaguars but retires with a broken wheel. Gurney is deeply disappointed to have the same car rejected for a Silverstone meeting later in the season. He suspects skulduggery.

Dan is seen at Laguna Seca in April 1970 in the first of four races that season in a Plymouth Barracuda in the Trans-Am Series. He retires the AAR-prepared car in all the races except the last one at Riverside in October at which he announces his retirement.

At Dan's urging Frank Arciero is an early customer for the Lotus 19 sports car, which indeed proves a strong performer. Gurney tweaks the throttle of its Coventry Climax engine during a warm-up at Riverside in October 1960 (left) and wins with it at Laguna Seca in October 1962 (above). In 1964 Dan steps out of the cockpit of the Ford-powered Lotus 19B (opposite, top) with which he has been leading the Nassau Trophy Race until his clutch gives way. Two months earlier in October 1964 (opposite, bottom) Dan drives the 19B to second at Laguna Seca. He is creating the nucleus of the team that in the following year will become All American Racers.

Dan Gurney could scarcely start the 1966 Can-Am season more decisively than he does at Bridgehampton in September with his Lola-Gurney-Weslake-Ford, starting from pole and winning outright on the demanding Long Island circuit. None could have imagined that this would be the only win for Ford and AAR in Can-Am history. With a bigger Weslake-Ford V-8 and a newer Lola Gurney contests the 1967 season. At Laguna Seca (overleaf) he qualifies second but retires early with overheating problems.

What a difference a day makes. The brand-new Olsonite McLeagle is pristine in practice for Bridgehampton in September 1968 but by race day is festooned with a slathering of decals. Its Eagle wheels bespeak the special attention its chassis has been given.

The McLeagle places sixth on its Bridgehampton debut (above). With 427 cubic inches of Chevrolet V-8 and a big rear wing it is a more potent proposition at Laguna Seca in October 1969 (below) and qualifies fourth fastest but retires with piston failure.

By rights Dan Gurney and AAR should own the Can-Am Series, but it ranks third in their priorities after Indy racing and Formula 1. Nor is Dan's engine supplier of choice, Ford, able to rival the clandestine efforts of Chevrolet. Dan is competing at Bridgehampton in 1968 (above) and at Las Vegas in November of the same year with a new Lola T160 (below). It breaks a half-shaft there and fails an engine at Riverside in October 1968 (opposite top).

Chief mechanic Wayne Leary makes a custom adjustment on the McLeagle in 1968 (below left) and Dan waits out the inevitable delays of practice at Bridgehampton (below right). For the 1970 Can-Am season Gurney sets aside his own programme and drives instead for McLaren until he concludes that the relationship is not rewarding enough for the frustrations it provokes. However, Gurney leaves an indelible mark at the wheel of the orange McLaren M8D with its 465-cubic-inch Chevrolet V-8 (overleaf).

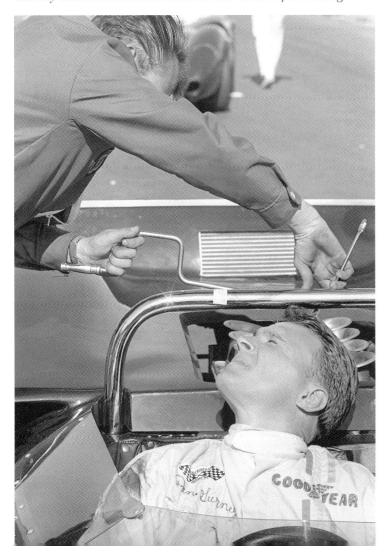

CHAPTER 8

Reigning at Riverside

The sensation of the first-ever race weekend at Riverside International Raceway east of Los Angeles was a young driver who was, wrote Jim Mourning, 'unheralded in pre-race publicity … turned in a performance … displaying remarkable ability and an almost brilliant grasp of racing tactics … that left the experts, both recognised and self-appointed, firmly convinced they had seen a future world champion in action.' His performance was, said Mourning, 'the main point of interest for the weekend.' And that sensational driver was … the 15-year-old Ricardo Rodriguez, in a Porsche Spyder, winning the 1500cc modified race.

'Though the race for production cars over 2000cc didn't stir the same excitement,' Mourning continued in *Sports Cars Illustrated*, 'Dan Gurney proved to be the

Dan Gurney's victory in 1966 in the NASCAR 500-mile race at Riverside is his fourth in succession – a record for that sanctioning body. His Ford is immaculately prepared and crewed by the Wood brothers. These are heartening successes for Gurney, who is then in the throes of setting up All American Racers. He scores no other victories between the Riverside stock-car contests of 1965 and '66.

class of the field as he scored one for Detroit by wheeling a Corvette to a 29-second win over the Mercedes-Benz driven by Jack Bates.' In the headlines after 22 September 1957 Dan had to play second fiddle not only to main-race winner Richie Ginther but also to precocious Mexican sensation Rodriguez. Later Gurney would garner more than enough post-Riverside headlines to make up for this slight.

The praise given to these drivers after Riverside's first race was well justified. This was no ordinary circuit. The brainchild of restaurateur and racer Rudy Cleye, the 3.3-mile track had been built in 528 rolling acres of near-desert terrain at a cost of $800,000. Funded by wealthy car owner and entrant John Edgar, it was intended to be a multi-purpose facility with a drag strip and oval track, though the latter never materialised. Even without its oval Riverside was Southern California's first major racing complex, designed to draw spectators from the entire region. With the help of major newspaper promotions, it did just that.

But Riverside, dubbed a 'little Nürburgring', was a wicked circuit. Jim Mourning again: 'Whether by accident or design, the layout contains nearly every nasty feature to be found in road racing circuits anywhere, including dips, changes in camber, decreasing-radius turns and a banked turn – *sans* escape route – on the end of the long straightaway. Even though no one really doubted the trickiness of the course or the sincerity of club officials when they practically begged for caution, the weekend record showed one casualty, one case still in doubt, one severely injured driver and a lot of badly bent machinery.'

Case in point: driving the Maserati 450S of track-backer John Edgar, Carroll Shelby was the main-race favourite. On his very first practice lap of the track Carroll crashed so severely into the embankment flanking turn six that he needed 70 stitches and minor plastic surgery to put his face together. Turn six, a tight rising and falling off-camber right-hander, also caused the weekend's fatality. The sinuous esses from the start-finish to turn six often left drivers wondering which turns they were on. And the steel wall on the outside of the fast right-hand turn nine was unforgiving of brake failure after the mile-long straight.

This was the track on which Dan Gurney had driven so brilliantly in Cal Bailey's black Corvette in his first race at Riverside. How had he so mastered this daunting circuit? 'I had never raced there but I knew the track. Skip Hudson and I had worked on segments. Turn nine, the last turn before the pits, was an important turn but it was a vague turn. You could enter it in a lot of different ways. There didn't seem to be any real decisive key to it. But I reckoned that we had a pretty good idea of how to do it. So doing that helped. But otherwise it was just settling down to driving.'

Gurney's preparation paid off. Jerry Austin, a successful Corvette racer, jumped into the lead but then spun off, tricked by Riverside. That left the way clear for Dan to win the race that qualified him not only to run in the main event as well but also to take the wheel of the Arciero Ferrari in the next event at Riverside on 17 November. 'Dan gave it the ride of its life,' wrote Carroll Shelby, who won that race with Gurney second. 'Boy, Dan Gurney might be a newcomer, but he sure as heck knew how to drive a race car!' Fortunately for Dan's career Shelby was generous in his praise of the novice, whose Ferrari was timed at 163.1mph on the long straight.

A year later, on 12 October 1958, Riverside's managers achieved their goal of inviting an international field of cars and drivers to compete in a professional event. They attracted as well a cohort of the best Indy-car drivers, among whom was Dan's friend Troy Ruttman. The race's early laps produced an epic battle between Phil Hill's Ferrari and Chuck Daigh's Scarab in what was billed as the United States Grand Prix for sports cars. Phil retired and second place behind Daigh was taken by Gurney in the Arciero Ferrari. He collected a much-needed $1,500 and another big boost to his reputation.

One of the sensations of the first Riverside 'Grand Prix' had been the Buick-powered 'Ol' Yaller' entered and driven by its builder, Max Balchowsky. A cross between a hot rod and a sports car, Ol' Yaller was a crude-looking piece of kit with fenders borrowed from a pick-up truck and white-sidewall tyres. This was just the kind of car that appealed to Dan's renegade sense of humour. He took its wheel for an April 1960 race at Riverside and placed it third on the grid. Engine trouble sidelined him in the race.

In time for the sports car Grand Prix in October 1960 Frank Arciero had taken delivery of the Lotus 19 that Dan had urged him to buy. But it was not the favoured mount at first, as Dan told Joe Scalzo: 'Frank had a Ferrari-Maserati special entered at Riverside besides the Lotus, and there was a pretty much common feeling that the Maser would be able to beat the Lotus easily. So at first the 19 didn't get all the attention it needed, and toward the end we turned ourselves into nervous wrecks trying to get it ready. It's different from a Ferrari, which is about 95 per cent ready when you get it. A Lotus is nearer 75 per cent.' In the end it wasn't quite ready. Dan put the Lotus on pole but retired. Nor was the Lotus-Climax up to snuff in the 1961 and '62 'Grand Prix' races.

In subsequent visits to his home circuit with sports-racing cars, Gurney was fated never to win a major race. With the Ford-powered Lotus 19B he set a practice lap record and won a preliminary race in October 1964 but retired with suspension trouble in the main event. In his Can-Am years he was a frequent pole-sitter but a finisher only once, fourth with his McLeagle-Chevy in 1969. Fortunately, Dan had compensations.

Thoughts for the future were triggered in the mind of

Riverside general manager Les Richter by Dan Gurney's maiden test of his new Indy Eagle in March 1966. Dan used a shorter 2.7-mile course, which left out a loop into the track's infield. The driver was exuberant about the prospects of using Riverside for a USAC championship event, saying that it offered excellent opportunities for passing almost anywhere on the circuit. Richter declared his intent to make that happen.

Happen it did, on 26 November 1967, and it produced a dilly of a race. It was the final USAC event in a season that had left the championship undecided between Mario Andretti and A. J. Foyt. Richter did an outstanding job of lining up a variegated field in the Riverside tradition for a race that was run in the usual clockwise direction, counter to USAC custom. Rounded up to join the usual USAC suspects were sports car specialists George Follmer, John Surtees, Ronnie Bucknum and Chuck Parsons. And none other than Jimmy Clark was making one of his rare non-Lotus appearances to drive a Vollstedt-Ford.

A different short course of 2.6 miles was used, one that usefully cut off a chunk of the long straight. Having tested at the track earlier in the week, Gurney skipped the first day of qualifying. Clark was fastest on Friday but when Dan arrived on Saturday he immediately captured an unbeatable pole in his Eagle powered by a Gurney-Weslake Ford. Clark was next to him in the front row, followed by John Surtees and Bobby Unser. Championship rivals Foyt and Andretti were in the third row for the rolling start.

The 300-mile race named for the late Rex Mays was memorably chaotic. It was described by one reporter as 'Mack Sennett-like', referring to frenetic silent-film comedies, and by another as 'wild and woolly'. Lloyd Ruby set the style by spinning half-way around the first lap with two-thirds of the charging field close behind him. Ruby not only recovered but went on to finish fourth. The second lap saw another spin and Bobby Unser hitting the wall at turn nine, but not severely enough to retire him.

Meanwhile Gurney shot into the lead 'with Clark not a foot off his backside,' said Del Owens in *Autoweek*. On the 23rd of 116 laps Clark passed Gurney on the inside in the treacherous turn six but Dan was soon

challenging again. A lap later Clark's engine, over-revved earlier, gave up the ghost and Jimmy waved Dan by.

After a mid-race fuel stop Dan was back in the lead and looking good. The 38,000 fans rejoiced as the pride of Riverside seemed set to score a welcome win. But on lap 72 they groaned as he swerved into his pit with a deflating right rear tyre. After a quick change, wrote Owens, 'the way the AAR driver went out of the pits, sideways, it was obvious he had not given up the race.' Now third, Dan was trailing the leading Andretti and Bobby Unser in another Eagle by more than a minute.

Dan started running two seconds a lap faster than Mario in his bid to catch the leader. He was 16 seconds behind with five laps to go when Andretti's engine sputtered and he had to pit for fuel. In turn nine, just before the white-flag lap, Gurney darted under new leader Unser to take first place. Dan was, understandably, described as 'jubilant' after this dramatic finish. Behind the battling leaders Foyt, finishing fifth in his second car of the day, collected just enough points to win an unprecedented fifth USAC championship.

Here was a race finish like the one that Dan described to Peter Manso: 'Suppose something happens towards the end of the race and the only hope I have of winning is to run it as hard as I can? In many respects it relieves you of the responsibility of trying to nurse the car along. And if it lets go under those circumstances, why, nobody can really criticise you.' This time his well-prepared Eagle didn't let go.

A rival team lodged a protest over Gurney's engine after the 1967 Rex Mays race, but an inspection showed its displacement to be only 301 cubic inches against an allowance of 305. Understandably Dan used a similar engine in a new Eagle for the Rex Mays 300 in December 1968. This race too produced a Gurney victory from pole. Dan contested his final Riverside USAC race in December 1969. He started from pole and finished third.

A similar abbreviated circuit was used for a series of NASCAR Grand National stock car races at Riverside. A prequel to these was a race there in March 1962 in which Dan drove his Chevrolet Impala. He was out with a disqualification. The stakes were raised in 1963 by *Motor Trend*'s sponsorship of a 500-mile NASCAR race on the 2.6-mile circuit. Again Riverside had wangled international recognition for the race so that drivers from other disciplines, like Foyt and Gurney, could drive against the NASCAR greats.

By January 1963, of course, Dan Gurney was firmly in the Ford camp. And Ford had a car for him, a Galaxie fastback with a 427-cubic-inch engine of more than 400 horsepower. As in his USAC debut at Riverside, Dan waited until the second day to make his qualifying bid. 'Work in other pits gradually stopped,' wrote Cutter and Fendell. 'Dixie mechanics as well as drivers from all over the country stood along pit row trying to look nonchalant. The stop watches were in many hands as Gurney crawled into his car.' He lapped a second and a half faster than his next quickest rival, although his second-day time meant that he would start 11th.

The 44 big, heavy cars that would take the rolling start at Riverside in front of 52,000 spectators were facing 500 miles of racing, 185 laps of America's most treacherous track. Gurney's home advantage was significant, both in terms of his knowledge of Riverside and his appreciation of the strategy required. 'In a Grand Prix race you can run just as hard as you do in your qualifications,' he told Peter Manso. 'But you cannot do this in a Riverside 500. You have to hold back a little bit since the brakes won't take it. You try to think of 500 miles as opposed to 100 miles, and you try to understand how much the car will take.

'Basically you have a plan going into the race,' Dan added, 'a pretty good idea of just about how fast you should go. And if that means that you're going to back off 100 yards sooner, you just attempt to stick to that. In the early laps you may have somebody going hell for leather and it looks as if he's not hurting his car. So then you have to decide – should I increase the pace or not?'

It also depended on just who that driver was, said Gurney. 'Sometimes you find yourself with a desire to have it out with a particular person, to set the record straight. You may be using poor judgement in terms of the car's lasting the race but you just want to put him down. The best put-down is getting across the line first. And of course, besides winning there's turning the fastest lap, which indicates something too and means a lot to drivers.'

At the 1963 Riverside start Dan was behind a posse of Pontiacs. He bided his time while some of the chargers wrecked their motor cars. Only 21 of the 44 starters would finish. Gurney moved into the lead, then pitted, and regained the lead on lap 101, never to lose it. 'It was an easy race,' he said afterward. 'I was told to keep the engine under 5,800rpm and I did easily.'

For next year's race Dan had a Ford prepared by the Wood brothers, top-ranked among the NASCAR car preparers and renowned for their pit-stop skills. The weather washed out qualifying so the cars lined up in the order they had been presented for technical inspection. Luckily Gurney was fourth. When tyres were changed after an early yellow the Wood brothers got Dan out in the lead, but he couldn't hold Richard Petty in a Plymouth with Chrysler's new 'hemi' engine. Before one-third distance was reached, however, Petty retired.

Dan led a one-two-three finish for Ford, but the celebrations were muted. Riverside had exacted a price from its stock car racers. Popular veteran Joe Weatherly had crashed into the boilerplate wall on the outside of turn nine. Injuries suffered because his harness was not properly fastened proved to be fatal – the first death in seven seasons for safety-conscious NASCAR.

Gurney did not ignore the message of this fatality. 'Danger occupies a very big part of your consciousness,' he said. 'Race driving is a form of brinksmanship, I suppose. First, you use your judgement to determine where the brink is. Then you use your skill to approach the brink and stay at that point. It's sort of like balancing along a cliff. You can walk 3 or 4 feet from the cliff and have no problem, but someone closer to the edge can beat you. You need judgement to tell you where the edge of the cliff is and skill to get there and stay within a given safety margin.

'If you go off half-cocked,' Gurney continued, 'you're going to hurt yourself for sure. If you use judgement and keep attuned and stay aware of the reality of it all, you've got a better chance than the other guy of not getting hurt. I am aware of the danger all the time I'm driving. I think a lot of drivers ignore reality as one way of doing it. Others may say: 'Well, I realise it, but I use my skill and judgement to avoid a serious problem.' And also, in the end, you have to use your ability. There really isn't an answer. When a runner like Jim Ryun breaks the mile record, does he enjoy the actual running? He probably enjoys being the record-holder but not getting there. Well, that's how I feel.'

Once again with Ford and the Wood brothers Dan Gurney came, saw and conquered at Riverside in 1965. Dan bested a challenge from another American hero, Junior Johnson, to set fastest time, although on the second day, so he started 11th. In his Mercury Parnelli Jones made the early running but soon expired. Gurney and Foyt then made a race of it until A. J. went over the turn nine embankment and took an unscheduled trip to Riverside Hospital.

Although David Pearson seized pole in the 1966 race, Gurney's 'prowess in a stock car on the California road course was such that he had most of the field psyched before the race started,' wrote Leo Levine. Junior Johnson, now a retired driver and team owner, said, 'We got about as much business bein' here as a one-legged man in an ass-kickin' contest.' Indeed, Gurney covered the 500 miles in 5 minutes over 5 hours to become the first driver to win a major NASCAR race four times running.

In 1967 the Wood brothers were in Parnelli Jones's corner instead of Dan's. 'I respect Parnelli Jones's prowess as a driver and I think he respects mine,' said Gurney, 'but each of us would also enjoy crossing that line first. He happens to be one of the tougher guys to race against and he's on the Firestone team. I'm on the Goodyear team and this creates a certain rivalry or competitiveness. It brings out a little added incentive.' Parnelli scored the Riverside victory in '67 but Gurney, with the Wood brothers again, was on pole and won the 500 in 1968, making it five wins in six starts. He tried again in 1969 but suffered an engine failure in his Mercury.

At Indianapolis in 1969 a rookie, Mark Donohue, showed an impressive turn of speed in his first visit to the Speedway. A film crew had the notion of talking to Mark and Dan to contrast the views of the newcomer and the veteran. 'Dan surprised me,' said Mark, 'by mentioning retiring. He was saying that he'd gotten a lot out of racing but he didn't know how much longer he could keep it up. He sounded really tired and worn down. I couldn't understand what he was talking about at the time. But later, when I was in the same boat, I could relate to his feelings. There he was – a somebody – and a nobody like me comes up who he can't get away from. We were running about the same speed. A lot goes through your mind when that starts to happen.'

Gurney had been thinking for some time of retirement, and in 1970 he made the decision. He told Phil Llewellin why: 'First of all, I knew I was pretty darned good. I could focus and turn the tap wide open for the length of a race probably as well as any of the guys I ran against. Even when I quit, I still had 90-plus per cent of whatever it takes to satisfy yourself, but in the end, unless you have it 100 per cent, you should stop. I can't think of anything worse than being a journeyman driver who's just doing it because he needs to make a living. So if you have only 99 per cent, you ought not to be doing it.'

Appropriately, Dan announced his retirement at Riverside. He started third and finished fifth in a Trans-Am race with a Plymouth Barracuda on 4 October 1970. 'I still love racing,' he told his friends and admirers. 'It is my whole life. I will remain very active in racing, but not as a driver. I am 39, and although there are many examples of athletes succeeding in competition beyond that age, I've found that I've been getting more and more interested in some of the other aspects of racing. I've been feeling the strain of a conflict between my broad interests in racing – from car building and preparation to race promotion – and the single-minded purpose required of a driver. Driving takes a good deal of concentrated effort both on and off the race track. To be as active in racing as I want to be would just dilute my effectiveness as a driver.'

There was a coda to the career of Dan Gurney the racing driver. His final Riverside 500 stock car race had been in 1970 with the Plymouth team, starting from pole and finishing sixth. Exactly a decade later he stepped back into the cockpit again, this time in a Chevrolet. 'I've been thinking about this for years,' he confessed. 'I'm just a fan of auto racing, and this sort of thing appeals to me. My wife doesn't like it,' Dan admitted, 'but she understands. I've been talking about it for a long time, and one time she said, "If you really want to do it, go ahead." I know she'd rather I didn't, and probably she didn't think I would when she said that.' Seventh place at the start was 'not too shabby,' as Gurney might have said, and he did well until sidelined by transmission trouble.

'Of course I wish I had won the Indianapolis 500 and the Formula 1 World Championship,' Dan reflected in looking back on his career, 'but you mustn't let things like that overwhelm you with grief. I know that the world, no matter how much you want to ignore it, involves a lot of luck – pure luck that is beyond your control. I know where those I raced against held me in their esteem, where I fit on the totem pole. That was far more important to me than anything else. I realised there were many guys that ended up winning championships that were not a bit better or faster than I was, but that's the way things worked out. A lot of them aren't here any more, and that certainly is a compensating factor. I ended up going to races where I was lonely, because a lot of the guys I enjoyed competing with or seeing at the races weren't there.'

One of the men that Dan measured himself against was Jimmy Clark. 'It's tough to get into a position to race with him,' Gurney said at the time. 'The one time I thought I had beaten Jimmy fair and square – at Spa in 1964 – I ran out of fuel. I did win in France and Mexico that year, but each time Clark had trouble. I also had to play second fiddle to Jimmy at Indianapolis in 1963, where we were both driving Lotuses. Fortunately he didn't race against me in the Riverside 500!'

After Jim Clark's funeral at Duns in Scotland Dan visited the Clark family home. As the senior Clark said his goodbyes at the door he said to Gurney, 'You know, Dan, Jim often told me that of all the men he ever raced against, he felt that you were his strongest competitor.' This remark had a profound impact on Dan: 'It destroyed me, really, in terms of my self-control. I was drowned in tears. To hear that from someone whose son had been killed and wasn't there any longer was more than I could cope with. For a long time I didn't say anything about it because I felt it was a private thing and I didn't want to utilise it to sort of glorify my driving ability or reputation, but it was certainly the biggest compliment I ever received.'

Nor were Dan's feelings about Clark quickly forgotten. A year later his mother received a telegram from California that read as follows: 'A year has passed and my thoughts are with Jimmy as so often during the past season. I miss him very much at all the circuits and I ask you please to accept my sincere feelings of sympathy in these sad days of April. Sincerely, Dan Gurney.'

In the intervening years Dan himself had become the yardstick of performance for up-and-coming drivers, as Mark Donohue said above. Donohue invited the retired Gurney to dinner when Mark was considering hanging up his helmet: 'From what he said, I got the impression that it was going to be harder than I anticipated. He liked to race as much as I did, and many times he wanted to get back in his Eagles to see what was happening. But we were also alike in the knowledge that we couldn't keep driving just because we enjoyed it. We had to keep winning or stop entirely. A person might say we were spoiled kids – if we couldn't win, we'd go home – and maybe that holds some water.'

Another competitor at Dan's last Trans-Am race was New Englander Sam Posey. 'For years,' wrote Sam, 'his mere presence at a race had made that race important to me, and his excellence had been an absolute against which I could compare myself and measure my improvement. It was hard to believe he would never race again.

'I felt very ambivalent about Dan's retirement,' Sam continued. 'It meant that many of his ambitions would go unrealised: he never won Indy; he was never World Champion. Without those achievements engraved in the history books Dan's record would never be the proper measure of his skill. But I knew that Gurney would be remembered long after this year's Indy winner or last year's World Champion has been forgotten. It occurred to me that like Charles Lindbergh, Gurney had a magic presence which transcended the arena of his accomplishments; like Lindbergh he was the Lone Eagle.'

The senior Gurney is on the left to greet his son in Victory Lane at Riverside following the first running of the Rex Mays 300-mile race in November 1967. Dan's testing of his Indy car at Riverside encourages the organisers there to think of mounting a road race for USAC competitors.

Dan drives the formidable Arciero Ferrari 4.9-litre special at Riverside in several guises. In October 1958 when he finishes second (above) it still has a provisional fibreglass body. The handsome Sutton-built aluminium body is ready for the 1959 season. Gurney is practising (below) for the October 1959 race at Riverside in which he struggles to restart the Ferrari on the grid and makes an unexpected trip to the hospital after being struck heavily from behind.

Dan pilots some peculiar machinery at Riverside. For Briggs Cunningham in October 1963 he drives a Genie-Ford with a vertical battery of exhaust pipes, retiring (above). Also Ford-powered is AAR's own McLaren-Elva (below), in which Gurney makes fleeting appearances in the October 1965 Los Angeles Times Grand Prix. In April 1960 Gurney has his only outing in Max Balchowsky's 'Ol' Yaller II' (overleaf). Its Buick V-8 doesn't last out the race.

Gurney's first race in the Climax-powered Lotus 19 of Frank Arciero is at Riverside in October 1960 (above). He retires with engine-related ailments as he also does at the same event with the same car two years later (below). He is responding to Porsche-driving Jo Bonnier's suggestion to pass on the left in the treacherous turn six.

Built expressly by Lotus for Dan's own team, the Ford-powered 19B is used for sprint events as well as endurance races. In October 1964 it is heading Bruce McLaren's eponymous car in turn six (above) and entering the left-hand turn one past the pits. Dan wins a preliminary event but fails in the final.

Near the end of the 1968 Can-Am season Dan and AAR hope to shock the all-conquering McLarens with a new Lola T160 powered by a 7-litre Ford V-8, introduced at Riverside. However, the engine is already smoking (below) after seven of the 62 laps. Earlier in the 1960s Dan confers with his team colleagues at Riverside (opposite) and in October 1963 takes the wheel of a Shelby team Cobra (overleaf). He is seen on his way to fourth place in the one-hour GT race in a fine Tronolone portrait.

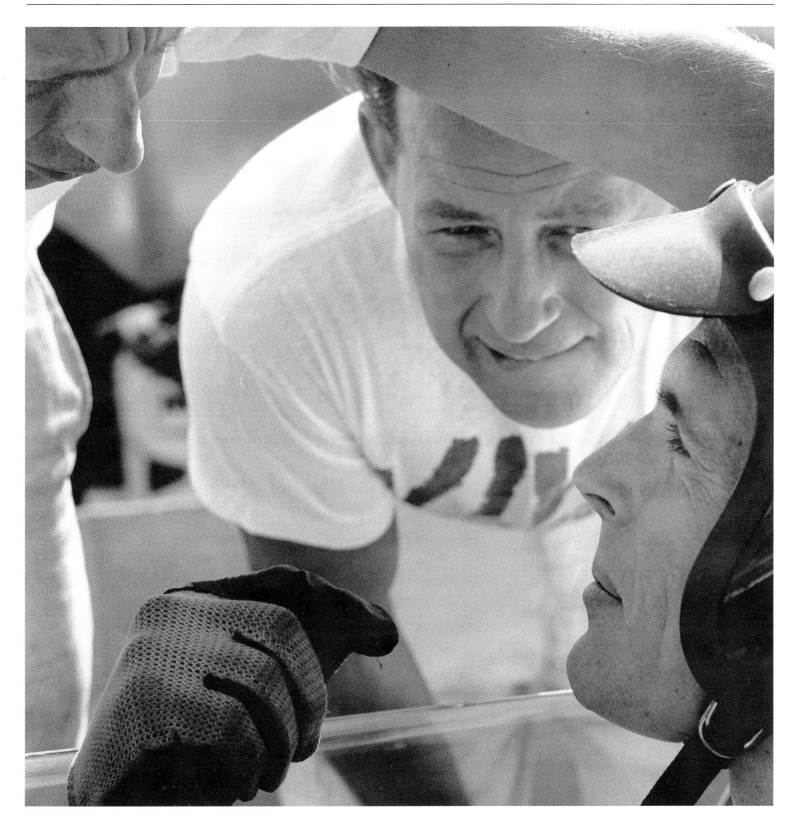

Dan Gurney's first stock car drive at Riverside is in a USAC 200-mile race in March 1962 at the wheel of a Chevrolet prepared by Bill Thomas. He is conferring with fellow driver Dave MacDonald (below left) and is joined by long-time friend Skip Hudson (below right). Dan suffers disqualification in the race.

In January 1967 at Riverside (above left) Dan chats with Bud Moore, for whom he will race a Mercury Cougar at Daytona a week later. With Bob Petersen, publisher of Motor Trend, *Dan celebrates his win in the 1966 500-mile stock car race at Riverside. He uses a 1966 Ford prepared by the Wood brothers (below) to bring home the cheque for $18,125.*

Bob Tronolone's portraits across these pages depict some of Gurney's Riverside stock cars. In 1967 he retires in the Mercury entered by Holman and Moody (16). In the white Ford (121) Dan scores his final Riverside stock-car victory in January 1968, again with the support of the Wood brothers. His Mercury Cyclone (121) suffers engine failure in 1969 and in 1970 he starts from pole and finishes sixth in a Petty-prepared Plymouth (42).

The combination of Dan Gurney, a Weslake-Ford-powered Eagle and the Riverside circuit is pure poison for the opposition. Dan leads from pole to win in December 1968 (above and opposite), bemusing the pursuing Mark Donohue who later admits that he forgot to pay attention to his own driving. With an Eagle Santa Ana (below) Gurney places third in the USAC race at the end of 1969. Dan wins the first such race in 1967 (overleaf), an event that sees him charging to the chequered flag from behind. This bespeaks the invincible character of one of the most determined and skilful racing drivers of all time.

Annotated Bibliography

Biro, Pete 'Dan Does It' (*Car and Driver*, September 1967)

Three pages covering the 1967 Belgian Grand Prix that Gurney won in his own car. The article title pretty well sums it up, the first time that an American had won a Grand Prix in an American car for 46 years. It still is.

Brabham, Jack *When the Flag Drops* (William Kimber, 1971). 240pp, 33 b/w photographs

The famously reticent Brabham actually told a good tale with a foreword by Graham Hill, which features favourable comments on Gurney who drove for 'Black Jack' for three seasons (1963-65). In fact Brabham had considered giving up driving during 1965 and running the team with DG and Denny Hulme for 1966, but of course Gurney wanted to do his own thing. Had he stayed on there is little doubt as to who would have been 1966 World Champion. This is Brabham's opinion as well.

Brawner, Clint and Scalzo, Joe *Indy 500 Mechanic* (Chilton Book Company, 1975). 194pp, 30 b/w photographs

Fascinating tale of American track racing and the characters who made it so unique. Brawner was a chief mechanic who worked for and knew most of the top drivers including the legendary Jimmy Bryan during his Dean Van Lines period. This book illustrates just how very different Indy racing was from contemporary European F1.

Claes, Cynthia *Autoweek*, 10 August 1992

Featured on the cover with a background picture of his 1967 Spa victory, Gurney is given the star treatment over six pages by Claes, Tim Considine and Sam Moses. The article covers his past, present and future, and reminds us of his motorcycle project code-named 'Alligator'.

Clew, Jeff *Lucky All My Life, The Biography of Harry Weslake* (Haynes, G. T. Foulis, 1979). 176pp, 96 b/w photographs plus numerous drawings and poster illustrations

Harry Weslake was an engineering polymath who designed and manufactured cylinder-head modifications, carburettors and whole engines for all and sundry including Bentley, Brough, Sunbeam, Riley, Alta, Norton, Jaguar, BRM and Coventry Climax amongst others, and of course the Gurney-Weslake V-12 for Dan Gurney's Eagle F1 car. Sadly a lack of finance and quality control of engine ancillaries led to Gurney leaving Weslake, from which the project never recovered. This is the story of a brilliant engineer who is most associated these days with motorcycles and speedway bikes.

Considine, Tim *American Grand Prix Racing, A Century of Drivers & Cars* (Motorbooks International, 1997). 196pp, 209 b/w and 29 colour photographs

It is surprising how many American drivers appear within the remit of this title, which is printed on very high quality art paper and covers all American participation in Grand Prix racing over the decades. Starting with George Heath in 1898 and ending with Michael Andretti in 1993, including the cars and races as well, this is a handsome volume let down by a number of errors that are listed on a separate sheet and some rather poor colour repro. However, it is a good reference source for arcane facts and figures and Gurney is well covered in text and pictures.

Cutter, Robert and Fendell, Bob *The Encyclopaedia of Auto Racing Greats* (Prentice-Hall Inc, 1973). 675pp, hundreds of b/w photographs

Vast pot pourri of racing biographies with Gurney rating nearly five pages. This is a good book for those lesser-known individuals whom you keep reading about but wonder who they were. Inevitably many are American track racers.

Crombac, Gerard ('Jabby') *Colin Chapman, The Man and his Cars* (Patrick Stephens Limited, 1986). 383pp, 242 b/w photographs

Magnum opus on Chapman by long-time friend and veteran French F1 writer 'Jabby' Crombac, who completely ignores the De Lorean scandal. The foreword is by Enzo Ferrari, no less! DG features with regard to the purchase of a Lotus 19, which was to be fitted with a Ford V-8, the mid-'60s Indy racing and the employment of Lotus designer Len Terry for Gurney's then new AAR team.

Davis, David E. Jr *Car and Driver*, July, August and November 1964

Three spoof articles in the Davis column 'From the Driver's Seat' suggest that Dan Gurney should stand for President of the USA and then announce his withdrawal in the last one. Although an obvious joke this is an indication of just how popular DG really was/is.

Davis, David E. Jr *Car and Driver*, September 1967

America victorious as Davis reports on Ford's Le Mans win with Gurney and an unlikely A. J. Foyt sharing the winning car in his 'The Twenty-Four Hours of Le Mans, or FORD BEATS FERRARI COLD HENRY POURS IT ON'. This was the famous occasion when Gurney apparently invented the champagne-spraying habit so beloved of latter-day F1. Elsewhere in the issue appears the Dutch Grand Prix, which Davis titles 'Ford Had a Better Idea'. This was the second Grand Prix appearance of the Eagle Weslake and DG practised second but stopped early on with fuel-injection problems.

Donohue, Mark with Van Valkenburgh, Paul *The Unfair Advantage* (Dodd, Mead & Company, 1975). 306pp, 35 b/w photographs

Donohue was the archetypal crew-cut American who truly deserved the sobriquet 'Captain America'. His painstaking approach was driven by a surprising amount of self-doubt but

his relationship with Roger Penske achieved much fame and fortune. His admiration and respect for Gurney are writ large in the book and later on in his career he drove Eagle Indy cars. Sadly Donohue died as a result of head injuries in 1975, after walking away apparently unharmed from a horrible crash during practice for the Austrian Grand Prix.

Finn, Joel E. *Maserati Birdcage, The marvellous Tipo 60 and 61 sports racing cars* (Osprey, 1980). 207pp, hundreds of b/w photographs plus graphs and cutaway drawing

An almost definitive work on the subject, which has heavy American content and is a must for Maser enthusiasts. Gurney features in his role as a Camoradi driver, which produced the famous 1960 Nürburgring 1,000 Km victory with Moss.

Gill, Barrie *The Men* (Leslie Frewin, 1968). 224pp, 55 b/w photographs

The author was one of the most prolific motor sports writers of the time and this is his look at the world of motor racing featuring 18 top drivers of the day including Gurney. It has some very good photographs that are wasted in the small format typical of such books, but gives a personal insight into the genre that was all too often lacking elsewhere.

Gurney, Dan '24 Heures Du Mans' (*Sports Cars of the World, 1971*). 2pp

Dan describes his 1967 Le Mans victory with A. J. Foyt in a magazine article, where he describes deliberately practising at a modest pace so as not to demoralise A. J. who was primarily an Indy car racer. Imagine anybody doing that now for a team-mate? I don't think so.

Gurney, Dan 'Dan' (*Car and Driver*, January 1971). 7pp, 19 b/w photographs and one line drawing

A photo article with captions by Gurney summarising his career and providing some telling comments. A couple of small mistakes appear in the final caption, but who cares?

Hamilton, Mike 'Dan Gurney, All American Champion' (*Automotive Shopping News*, 4 November 1970)

Promotional article in a trade newspaper celebrating Gurney's career and his recent retirement at the age of 39.

Henry, Alan *Driving Forces – Fifty men who shaped the world of motor racing* (Patrick Stephens Limited, 1992). 200pp, 74 b/w photographs

As its title suggests, a brief look at the lives of various motor sport icons, drivers, constructors, entrants, team managers, officials, designers, engine builders, etc. Each subject is given a neat if necessarily superficial write-up in the typical Henry style.

Hill, Graham *Life at the Limit* (William Kimber, 1969). 255pp, 34 b/w photographs

One of many almost formulaic period autobiographies from this publisher, which reminds us that Dan Gurney actually won a race in a BRM, his last for Bourne in fact, at Ballarat in Australia in 1961. Completed just after Hill's 1969 Watkins Glen shunt, the book reveals Graham's misguided determination to carry on despite already failing powers. His final words tellingly are 'I must be thankful that the accident occurred at the end of a season and I did not miss too many races'.

Kistemaker, Dale and Smith, Kent James *Passion and Precision: the Photographer and Grand Prix Racing 1894-1984* (The Long Beach Museum of Art, 1984). 119pp, 112 photographs

A wonderful collection of interviews with famous photographers (Klemantaski, Cahier, Alexander, Schlegelmilch, Snowden, etc), journalists (Lamm, Molter, etc), editors and authors (Guichard, Ludvigsen, etc) and of course drivers (Brabham, Dreyfus, Gurney, Phil Hill, Moss, etc), all as part of an exhibition of Grand Prix photography at the time. Gurney is in reflective mood about not winning the World Championship or Indianapolis, and who remembers that it was he who supplied the title for Robert Daley's famous book *The Cruel Sport*?

Lawrence, Mike *Brabham, Ralt, Honda – The Ron Tauranac Story* (Motor Racing Publications, 1999). 256pp, 44 b/w photographs, 16 colour photographs and 3 cutaway drawings

As enigmatic and taciturn as his famous partner, Ron Tauranac is a man of few words but strong opinions and this is a story well told by the author. Gurney is rated highly and the very valid point is made that Dan's large size and relatively heavy weight placed him at a possible disadvantage in the tiny 1½-litre F1 cars. Comment is also made about the need to pander to Gurney's penchant for mechanical adjustments, whilst actually doing nothing. Thus reassured, Dan would perform satisfactorily.

Levine, Leo *Ford: The Dust and The Glory – A Racing History* (The Macmillan Company, New York, 1968). 630pp, hundreds of b/w photographs

A vast tome with the accent firmly on America and the extraordinary track racing that took place there over the decades. Largely forgotten or even unknown in Europe was Gurney's very successful interlude in NASCAR racing for the legendary Wood brothers. Levine is said to be at work on an updated version.

Litsky, Frank *The New York Times*, 24 June 1967

A newspaper article featuring DG, his life and times and describing him as the man to beat in World Championship

races. This interview was written in London a few days after Dan had won the Belgian Grand Prix and goes on to describe his attitude to danger and the $150,000-$200,000 of life insurance that he carried.

Llewellin, Phil 'The Racer's Racer' (*Automobile*, April 1995). 6pp, 11 b/w and 6 colour photographs

Well illustrated and researched article that notes Gurney's respect for and interest in the history of motor sport. His admiration for the Nürburgring, Rouen, the Targa Florio and the great drivers from the 1950s are significant. He also wanted to race in the Mille Miglia and the Carrera Panamericana, which he described as challenges you could really sink your teeth into.

Lyons, Pete *Can-Am* (Motorbooks International, 1995). 268pp, 301 b/w and 50 colour photographs plus fully tabulated results

Superb, definitive large-format (like this one) book on all the Can-Am racers of the 1960s and '70s with a wealth of photographs and detailed history of the venues, cars, entrants and drivers. Gurney's Can-Am racing was spasmodic due to conflicting priorities, but he did win once in 1966 and then twice in 1970 for McLaren at the end of his career.

Manso, Pete *Vroom!! – Conversations with the Grand Prix Champions* (Funk & Wagnalls, New York, 1969). 227pp, 105 b/w photographs

Despite the comic-style title, a very interesting book on the thoughts and beliefs of ten drivers including DG. Manso asks some searching questions of Gurney about safety, death and associated problems. They also stray into politics, civil rights and hippies, whom Gurney regards as a bunch of phoney bat shit! Thankfully there is plenty of racing amongst the social angst of the day, all of which occupies some 20 pages.

McNamara, Steve 'Dan Gurney' (*Sports Cars Illustrated*, April 1960). 10pp, 6 b/w photographs

An early article by a contemporary American magazine as Gurney's European racing took off properly and his claim to international fame grew. It gives an interesting insight into the *modus operandi* of Ferrari in 1959 and Phil Hill's comments about Gurney being impatient. Mention is made of DG's many licence endorsements for speeding in California and his subsequent calming down. Sounds familiar.

Nixon, Christopher 'Profile – Dan Gurney' (*Autosport*, 20 November 1959). 2pp, 5 b/w photographs

These days a highly acclaimed author and then an *Autosport* staffer, Chris Nixon takes a look at Gurney's first foray into European racing. As with so many others Nixon talks of Gurney's World Championship potential, which, alas, was to be frustrated.

Nolan, William F. 'Dan Gurney: California Challenger' (*Sportscar Graphic*, May-June 1960). 5pp, 4 b/w photographs

Another of the early articles capturing Gurney's rapid, indeed meteoric, rise to fame during 1958-59 and the preceding years.

Nye, Doug *Great Racing Drivers* (Hamlyn Publishing Group, 1977). 156pp, hundreds of b/w and colour photographs

A superior potboiler from Doug Nye that covers the years between 1900 and 1976 and some of the drivers who excelled during that time. The text is limited and each subject, including Gurney, is given a brief potted history, but there are plenty of pictures to compensate, although by modern standards the matt paper is a little utilitarian.

Nye, Doug *BRM Volume 1 – Front engined cars 1945-1960* (Motor Racing Publications, 1994). Hundreds of b/w photographs and 17 colour photographs, assorted cutaway and line drawings and fully tabulated results and chassis numbers

The award-winning BRM book from Nye must rate as one of the best one-make books ever, apart from its irritating lack of an index. Gurney is given a brief mention by Peter Spear of BRM who thought him remarkably promising. His comments about Gurney's height not being suitable for the smaller cars coming in 1960/61/62, which will favour the smaller man, echo similar sentiments elsewhere. DG went on to become a BRM driver in 1960 but did not enjoy the experience.

Phipps, David 'Dan Gurney – All American Racer' (*The Encyclopaedia of Super Cars, Volume 10, Issue 118*, Orbis Publishing, 1993). 5pp, 6 b/w and 14 colour photographs plus 5 colour profiles

Nicely illustrated piece by photojournalist David Phipps summarising Gurney's career and some of the more notable cars he drove. Published as part of a special series by Orbis.

Roche, Murray 'Get out of the way for old Dan Gurney' (*Road & Track*, October 1959). 4pp, 4 b/w photographs

A rather inappropriately titled article (DG was 28 at this time) that covers the formative years and his arrival in Europe.

Roebuck, Nigel 'Legends' (*Motor Sport*, November 1998). 2pp, 2 photographs

F1 authority Roebuck talks to Gurney about his early days against the backdrop of the 1998 Goodwood Revival meeting where Dan showed his true enthusiasm for all things mechanical – cars, bikes and planes.

Scalzo, Joe 'Gurney talks to CP' (*Competition Press & Autoweek*, 29 January 1966).

A pre-season look at Gurney's plans for the then new 3-litre F1, which rather optimistically cites four cars! Jerry Grant was to be the No 2 and mention is made prematurely of the 400bhp Weslake engine. The reality was to be somewhat more modest and behind schedule.

Schuler, Steve *Dan Gurney Racing Career Review Reports*. 23pp

A fully tabulated and annotated list of Gurney's racing career compiled for this book project, giving venue, date, cars driven, results and/or reasons for retirement. A superb source of information that is highly recommended.

Small, Steve *The Grand Prix Who's Who* (Guinness Publishing Ltd, 1996, 2nd Edition). 464pp, hundreds of b/w portraits

A detailed reference work on every Grand Prix driver and the cars they drove from the inception of the F1 World Championship in 1950 to date of publication. Gurney is on pages 188/189.

Stanley, Louis *Grand Prix. The Legendary Years – The Personal Memoirs of Louis Stanley* (Queen Anne Press, 1994). 248pp, hundreds of b/w photographs

Always controversial and sometimes surprisingly astute, his stated opinions of Gurney are perhaps more perceptive than is obviously apparent.

Yates, Brock *Sunday Driver* (Farrar, Straus & Giroux, New York, 1972). 258pp, 11 b/w photographs

Famous author and *Car and Driver* editor Yates tells the story of his odyssey to become a competent driver by enrolling in Bob Bondurant's racing school at Ontario. The book contains an amusing anecdote of how Gurney was prevailed upon to perform a 'bootleg turn', better known in the UK as a handbrake turn, on a public road in a very unwieldy Chrysler Imperial Brougham. Yates of course also shared a Ferrari Daytona with Gurney on the first 'Cannonball' run from coast to coast in America.

Photograph credits

Jesse Alexander: P62 lower left; P63 upper right; P100; P101; P109 upper right; P121; P123; P125 upper; P128-129; P130 upper left; P189; P200.

Pete Biro: P196 upper left & upper right.

Bernard Cahier: P10; P17; P18 left; P22; P23 lower; P24 upper & lower; P26-27; P28 upper & lower; P29 left; P42; P54; P55 lower left; P57 left; P58 lower left; P59 upper & lower right; P60-61; P62 upper left & lower right; P64 upper; P65 upper & lower; P66-67; P69; P99 lower; P102 lower; P113; P114; P130 upper right & lower left; P141; P146-147; P163 upper; P193 upper right.

Alexis Callier: P52 lower left; P56 upper; P63 lower right; P102 upper; P103 lower; P145 lower left.

Éric della Faille Collection (Alexis Callier): P25.

Edward Eves from Ludvigsen Library: P63 upper left.

Dan Gurney Collection: P44; P52 upper left; upper right & lower right; P53 upper and lower; P98 upper; P122 upper & lower.

Max Le Grand from Ludvigsen Library: P108 lower left & lower right; P109 upper left; P112; P131 right; P145 upper; P148-149; P151 lower.

Karl Ludvigsen from Ludvigsen Library: P37; P84 upper left; P92 left & right; P93; P94 upper right; P95 lower right; P107 lower; P109 lower right; P130 lower right; P132 lower; P132-133 upper; P144 upper & lower left; P150 upper & lower; P151 upper; P152; P159; P164 left & right; P168 upper & lower; P169 upper; P172-173; P188 lower.

Ludvigsen Library Limited: P87 lower; P98 lower; P99 upper, P134, P142; P160 upper.

Günther Molter: P55 upper & lower right; P57 upper right & lower right; P58 upper right & upper left; P59 lower left; P124; P125 lower; P145 lower right.

Phipps Photographic: P23 upper; P29 right; P51 upper & lower; P56 lower; P58 lower right; P59 upper left; P62 upper right; P64 lower; P68; P80 upper left & right; P143; P148; P160 lower.

Stanley Rosenthall from Ludvigsen Library: P2; P9; P18 right; P19 upper & lower; P63 lower left; P70; P78 upper left, upper right, lower left & lower right; P79 upper, center & lower; P81 lower right; P84 upper right, lower left & lower right; P85; P86 upper left, upper right, lower left & lower right; P87 upper; P94 lower right; P95 upper left and upper right; P103 upper; P106; P107 upper; P109 lower left; P126 upper left, upper center, upper right, center left, center, center right, lower left, lower centre, lower right; P127 upper, lower left & lower right; P131 left; P133 lower; P144 lower right; P165 upper left, upper right, lower left & lower right; P170 upper left & upper right; P171 lower left & lower right.

Jim Sitz: P162 lower.

Judy Stropus: P108 upper left.

Bob Tronolone: P20-21; P30; P38 upper & lower; P39 upper & lower; P40-P41; P43; P77; P80 lower; P81 lower left & upper; P82-83; P88-89; P90 upper & lower; P91 upper & lower; P94 upper left & lower left; P95 lower left; P96; P97; P104-105; P108 upper right; P110 upper & lower; P111 upper & lower; P161 upper & lower; P162 upper; P163 lower; P166-167; P169 lower; P170 lower; P171 upper; P174; P181; P182 upper & lower; P183 upper & lower; P184-185; P186 upper & lower; P187 upper & lower; P188 upper; P190-191; P192 upper, lower left & lower right; P193 upper left & lower; P194 upper & lower; P195 upper & lower; P196 lower; P197; P198-199.

Index